MANUAL FOR (RELATIVELY) PAINLESS MEDICAL SPANISH

MANUAL FOR (RELATIVELY) PAINLESS MEDICAL SPANISH

A Self-Teaching Course

Ana Malinow Rajkovic, M.D.

 University of Texas Press, Austin

Requests for permission to reproduce material from this work should be sent to
Permissions, the University of Texas Press, Box 7819, Austin, TX 78713-7819.

(∞) The paper used in this publication meets the minimum requirements of American
National Standard for Information Sciences—Permanence of Paper for Printed Library
Materials, ANSI Z39.48-1984.

For reasons of economy and speed this volume has been printed from camera-ready
copy furnished by the author, who assumes full responsibility for its contents.

LIBRARY OF CONGRESS CATALOGING-IN-PUBLICATION DATA

Malinow Rajkovic, Ana, date.
    Manual for (relatively) painless medical Spanish : a self-teaching course / Ana
Malinow Rajkovic. — 1st ed.
        p.   cm.
    ISBN 0-292-75146-X (alk. paper : pbk.)
    1. Spanish language—Conversation and phrase books (for medical personnel).
2. Spanish language—Textbooks for foreign speakers—English.   3. Medicine—
Terminology.   I. Title.
    [DNLM: 1. Medicine—phrases—Spanish.   W   15   M251m]
PC4120.M3M34   1992
468.3'421'02461—dc20
DNLM/DLC
for Library of Congress   91-47543

To my husband, Aleks, and my son, Andrei.

Contents

Introduction

You have just spent good money on a catchy title, hoping that the old maxim "you can't judge a book by its cover" will not hold this time. After all, you have bought many a dreary-sounding-titled book, only to find out that it certainly was dreary! So why can't a funny-sounding book **be** funny?

Well, not exactly funny, but at least not tedious. We are going to learn medical Spanish, which does not lend itself to hilarity too readily. But we shall try.

The purpose of the textbook is to teach you how to communicate with your Spanish-speaking patient. What? You bought this thinking you were going to learn a few words in Spanish before you left for Club Med? Well, who knows, someone might choke on their Chile Rellenos, and you'll be glad you bought this after all! By the end of the book, you will be able to speak Spanish well enough to make yourself understood to your patients and to understand what they are saying back to you (but not if they speak Tagalog; you'll have to get a different book for them).

How will you accomplish this in the next few hundred pages? First, I entreat you to find a pencil (between the sofa cushions is a good place to look) or to buy one. This is not the "in-one-ear-out-the-other" method of learning Spanish. For maximal performance, you should fill in all the blanks, with your new pencil, in full sentences. If I ask you "¿Dónde está la ciudad de San Francisco?" ("Where is the city of San Francisco?") don't just write "California," write, "La ciudad de San Francisco está en California." Then check your answers against answers in the back of the book, correct them, and say everything written in Spanish out loud!! If people around you laugh, take it in stride, after all, you took French in high school, right?

So now that you are equipped with a pencil and are ready to fill in all the blanks in full sentences and say everything out loud, what's next? You will soon notice that you are going to learn Spanish the same way you would learn to build a house with blocks. First come the blocks for the foundation upon which everything else is built. Once you build the foundation, you will get a few blocks to put over the foundation, first one way, then another by using slightly different combinations and new blocks. For example, once you learn the "cornerstone" question "Do you have?" you can quickly learn "Do you have diarrhea?" "Do you have diarrhea with blood?" "Do you have diarrhea with blood after you eat?" and "For how long have you had diarrhea with blood after you eat?" The "cornerstones" start simply and progress, without your noticing, to greater difficulty, so that by the end of each lesson, you will understand all the new vocabulary, and all the new grammar, painlessly!

Popular methods to teach languages try not to use English. This is good and well if students already know Spanish or, if they don't know English. I like to think I strike a balance: first I make you sweat it out in Spanish, and when you're ready to throw the book out the window, I explain in English. Many of you are of a compulsive nature and have to understand every sentence before you go on to the next. This will not do. There will be many sentences, nay, whole paragraphs, that you will not understand immediately. But I promise you that everything is explained in good time. Trust me.

Often, I write English sentences as literal translations of the Spanish. For example, "Goes the boy sick to the room small?" Seeing the unusual order in English will remind you of the normal syntax in Spanish. For those of you trying to learn medical English, please see if you can't get your money back.

I might as well tell you now, before you tear up that receipt, that you will have to do a fair amount of memorizing. This, of course, is an anathema to anyone in the medical profession, I know. But the Spanish, being so clever, made up a different word in Spanish for every word in English! Well, not quite, because the god of grammar was good and saw fit to create "cognates," similar, or identical words in both languages. For example, words ending in -ion, -ble, -sis, and -itis are frequently the same in English and Spanish. We haven't even started and already you know how to say hospitalization, operable, acidosis, and pancreatitis in Spanish! As a matter of fact, you could sound quite fluent if you manage to speak in sentences with words ending with these suffices.

Another hint: if you have a choice between a word in English with a Latin root (i.e., urticaria) or an Anglo-Saxon root (i.e., hives), choose the Latin one. This becomes problematical if you don't know the difference, in which case, I suggest you add an -o or an -a to the end of the English word and wait for a response. Medicamento and doctora are good examples. Shouldero and necko are not.

One other suggestion, and then we'll get on with the show. That is: break down. Not personally, although you might feel like it at any point from now on, but your language. Take what you want to say in medical English and break it down into basic (i.e., lay) English. This can be translated into the basic Spanish you will learn. Your patients don't want to hear a symposium on the regression of atherosclerosis, they just want to know how many eggs they can eat a week.

The textbook, as you'll soon find out, is made up of twelve lessons. Each section of the lesson is headed by a "Vocabulary and Stress Guide" which should help you with vocabulary for that section and pronunciation. Each lesson closes with a bilingual interview which includes the vocabulary and grammar introduced in the lesson. Obviously, as you progress in the book, so does the difficulty of the interviews. Thus, the interview at the end of Lesson 1 will be the simplest, while the interview from Lesson 12, the most complex.

Interviews which close each lesson include: The Family Practice Clinic; The Emergency Room; Appendicitis; The Social Chat; The Pregnant Woman; The Family Planning Clinic; Pelvic Inflammatory Disease and Urinary Tract Infection; Depression; A Child with Asthma; The Patient with Angina; How to Explain a Venipuncture and a Spinal Tap; and A Patient with Congestive Heart Failure.

In the Appendix, you will notice a complete History and Physical Exam in English and Spanish, as well as lots of specialized vocabulary. Some of you might want to skip the first few hundred pages and turn right to that section, and memorize it by heart.

Sounds like a great vacation, doesn't it? It would be much funner, undoubtedly, to spend four weeks learning intensive Spanish in Guadalajara... but what do you expect for this price? Well, put on your hard-hat, grab that pencil, and let's get started!

Many special people have been instrumental in the inspiration, writing, editing, and, finally, publishing, of this book. I would like to thank the following people and institutions: my medical Spanish students, particularly those in the Department of Internal Medicine at San Francisco General Hospital and those in the Department of Family Medicine; the students at the University of California at San Francisco School of Medicine and at Case Western Reserve University and their respective universities, as well as other private funding organizations in the San Francisco area; Shannon Davies, Science Editor at the University of Texas Press and the reviewers of the first draft of the book; the Berlitz School of Languages in San Francisco; the department of Pediatrics at Rainbow Babies and Childrens Hospital; and finally, my family: my mother, for supplying me the original "Room of My Own"; my father, for the careful reading and editing of all my writing; and my in-laws, for watching over Andrei while I wrote this book.

Ana Malinow Rajkovic
Cleveland, 1991

MANUAL FOR (RELATIVELY) PAINLESS MEDICAL SPANISH

Lesson 1. Nouns

1.1 PRONUNCIATION

What does **ghoti** sound like? George Bernard Shaw said it was one way to spell *fish*. How? Take the **gh** of enou**gh** and you get *f*; the **o** of w**o**men and you get *i*; the **ti** of na**ti**on and you get *sh*: put them all together and you spell *fish*. In Spanish, there would be one and only one way to pronounce **ghoti** (like the small beard worn by Van Dyck), because in Spanish, we pronounce every letter, and with rare exceptions, each letter has only one way of being pronounced.

So how are the letters in Spanish pronounced? First, almost all consonants are pronounced the same way in English and Spanish. Second, when pronouncing any vowel, do not change the position of your mouth. Third, remember to open your mouth wide: you cannot have marbles in your mouth when you speak Spanish (you will have to find another place for them).

1.1.1 The Vowels

A   Open your mouth with jaw hanging down. Take index finger and pull down hard on bottom set of teeth (or equivalents). Don't stick out your tongue, but make the same sound you would when the doctor says to open wide and say: **aaaaaaaaaaaah.**
Pronounce: la da va sana mama papa

E   Say st**e**m. Now go back and only say st**e**. Now only say t**e**. Now only say **e.** Don't move your lips. You should look like a rabid dog with your nose a little gathered at the bridge.
Pronounce: te fe se de me sed red

I   Pinch your cheeks with both hands (like your aunt used to do when you were little) and pull your cheeks out with your fingers. Your lips should be stretched out, about 1/2 inch apart. Now make a sound. It can only be the **i** like in salam**i**.
Pronounce: mi si pis mis iris

O   It is imperative that your lips do not change their position for this vowel. So, with right hand, join thumb and index finger into a circle. Place the circle over your mouth and make your lips fit into the same circle. Push circle hard against lips. Say kn**o**t. Say n**o**t. (Isn't English strange?) Say **o**t. Say **o**. It can only be **o**.
Pronounce: no bobo coco mono loco poco

U   Pucker your lips. Pretend someone's rubbing your back. Now say **uuuuuuuuuuu**.
Pronounce: tu su sus sub pus lupus

N.B. **u** is silent in the groups **-que, -qui** and **-gue, -gui** unless it bears a diaresis.

1.1.2 The Consonants

Keep the following simple rules in mind when pronouncing consonants:

1. The only consonants that are doubled in Spanish are **c** (a**cc**idente) and **r** (Inglate**rr**a) and rarely **n** (i**nn**oble).
2. **ch** is always pronounced like **ch**ocolate and is considered as a separate letter found between "c" and "d" in the dictionary.
3. **g** sounds like **wh**ole in front of **e** or **i**; **g**eneral becomes **wh**eneral (or **ch**eneral for those of you who know how to pronounce **ch**utzpah, **ch**allah and le**ch**aim) and **g**in**g**ivitis becomes **wh**in**wh**ivitis (or **ch**in**ch**ivitis).
   g sounds like **g**o in front of **a, o, u**, as in **g**ato, **g**oma, or **g**usto.
4. **h** is never pronounced.
5. **j** follows the same rules a **g** above.
6. **ll** sounds like **i**; po**ll**o becomes po**i**o, costi**ll**a becomes costi**i**a.
7. **ñ** sounds like the **ny** of can**y**on; ni**ñ**o becomes ni**ny**o.
8. **v** is pronounced like **b**.
9. **z** sounds like **s** (except in Spain).

1.1.3 Tonic Stress and Written Accents

If there is no written accent over the word, how do you know where to put the stress? For example, how do you know that the stress in Acapulco is over the penultimate syllable, and not over the last? That loco is loco and not loco? That in Spanish, doctor is doctor and not doctor? Because there are rules, that's why.

Stress falls on the penultimate syllable if the word ends in a vowel, -n, or -s. Stress falls on the final syllable if the word ends in a consonant other than -n or -s. Thus, espalda, hermano, permanente, apendicitis, and toman; but dolor, hospital, nariz, and enfermedad.

It's much easier, of course, when there is a written accent, then you don't have to worry about knowing what penultimate is or how to find that syllable. An accent is used to break any of the above tonic stress rules. Stress over the final syllable of a word ending in a vowel requires an accent, thus café. Stress over the penultimate syllable of a word ending in a consonant needs an accent, thus lápiz. Best is to hope that words have written accent marks, so you can stress that syllable, but if not, remember that words ending in vowels have their penultimate syllable stressed, that words ending in consonants have their final syllable stressed, that -n and -s act like vowels, and that penultimate means next-to-the-last.

For those of you who were not daunted by the above section, read on.

1.1.4 Diphthongs

A diphthong is not summer footwear, rather, it is two vowels put together to make one syllable. Vowels are either "strong" (**a,e,o**) or "weak" (**i,u**). Tonic stress falls on the "strong" vowel, or on the second vowel if both are "weak." Thus, pie, cuarto, and cuello. Note that both vowels are pronounced. There are exceptions, and these are indicated with written accents.

1.1.5 Other Uses of Accent Marks

Words with identical spelling but different meaning are differentiated by written accents: **el** (the) and **él** (he); **si** (if) and **sí** (yes); **que** (that) and **qué** (what); **se** (oneself) and **sé** (I know).

And you thought that this was the **easy** part!

Let's have some fun. Just read the following in Spanish:

Los herpes son llagas que parecen como ampollas sin líquido, o una inflamación pequeña. La primera indicación que usted va a notar es una sensación de ardor o de picazón con dolor. Estas llagas pueden aparecer en muchas partes, inclusive los genitales exteriores, los muslos, el perineo, (área entre la vagina y el ano), el ano, o en las nalgas.

_____
_____
_____
_____
_____

Now, go back and underline all the words that sound similar in English (cognates). I found 21, not counting words that appear twice. Write their English meaning and try to decipher the paragraph. (You can at least make out that it's got something to do with herpes, right?)

1.2 INTRODUCTIONS

VOCABULARY AND STRESS GUIDE   (stressed syllables are underlined)

nouns (in order of appearance)

el doct<u>o</u>r	the doctor, m
la doct<u>o</u>ra	the doctor, f
la <u>ma</u>dre	the mother
el <u>pa</u>dre	the father
la profe<u>so</u>ra	the professor, f
el hospit<u>al</u>	the hospital
el <u>ni</u>ño	the boy
la <u>ni</u>ña	the girl
el estudi<u>an</u>te	the student, m
el paci<u>en</u>te	the patient, m
el medica<u>men</u>to	the medication

verbs

me <u>lla</u>mo	my name is
se <u>lla</u>ma	his/her/its name is

personal pronouns

yo	I
él	he
ella	she
usted	you, formal

proper names
Pepe
Juan
Ana
Rosa
Juana
Roberto
Felisa

expressions

Buenos días	Good day
Buenas tardes	Good afternoon
Buenas noches	Good evening/night
yo me llamo	my name is
él se llama	his name is
ella se llama	her name is
usted se llama	your name is
se llama	it's name is/it's called

interrogatives

¿Cómo se llama usted?	What's your name?

Buenos días.
Buenos _____
_____ días.
¡_____ _____ Pepe!
¡_____ _____ Juan!
¡_____ _____ Ana!
Buenas tardes.
Buenas _____
_____ tardes.
¡_____ _____ Pepe!
¡_____ _____ Juan!

Buenas noches.
Buenas _____
_____ noches.
¡_____ ____ Juan!
¡_____ ____ Ana!

Ana: **Yo me llamo Ana.**
Pepe: Yo me llamo Pepe.
Juan: Yo me llamo Juan.

El doctor **se llama** Vásquez.
La doctora se llama Gómez.
La madre se llama Rosa.
El padre se llama Ramón.

¿La madre se llama Juana?   No, la madre no se llama Juana.
¿La madre se llama María?   No, la madre no se llama María.
¿Cómo se llama la madre?   La madre se llama Rosa.
¿Cómo se llama el padre?   El padre se llama _____.
¿Cómo se llama el doctor?   _____Vásquez.
¿Cómo se llama la doctora?   _____Gómez.
¿Cómo se llama la profesora?   _____Ana.
¿Cómo se llama el hospital?   _____.
¿Cómo se llama el niño?   _____Roberto.
¿Cómo se llama la niña?   _____Felisa.
_____ la madre?   La madre se llama Rosa.
_____ el padre?   El padre se llama Ramón.
_____ _____ ?   El niño se llama Roberto.
_____ _____ ?   El doctor se llama Vásquez.
_____ _____ ?   La doctora se llama Gómez.
_____ usted?   Yo me llamo Ana.
_____ ?   Yo me llamo Ana.

Pepe: **¿Cómo se llama usted?**
Juan: Yo me llamo Juan. ¿Cómo se llama
                                        usted?
Pepe: Yo me llamo Pepe.

Ana: ¿Cómo se llama usted?
Estudiante: _____ ¿Cómo se llama
                                        usted?
Ana: Yo me llamo Ana.

Dr:	¿Cómo se llama usted?
Paciente:	_____ José. _____?
Dr:	Yo me llamo Doctora Gómez.
Dr:	¿Cómo se llama el hospital?
Paciente:	El hospital se llama _____.
Dr:	¿Cómo se llama el medicamento?
Paciente:	_____ Lasix.

If you think you are going crazy, you're not. In Spanish, we do not say "My name is ..." Instead, we say, "I call myself...," "you call yourself...," "he calls himself...," "she calls herself...," and "it calls itself..."

yo me llamo	**my name is**
usted se llama	**your name is**
él se llama	**his name is**
ella se llama	**her name is**
se llama	**its name is**

By the way. Did you read the *Introduction* ? No one ever does, that's why I didn't say anything important, but there are some funny lines.

1.3 WHAT?

VOCABULARY AND STRESS GUIDE

nouns (in order of appearance)

el <u>bra</u>zo	the arm
el <u>co</u>do	the elbow
el <u>de</u>do	the finger
el <u>o</u>jo	the eye
el <u>la</u>bio	the lip
el cu<u>e</u>llo	the neck
el estómago	the stomach
el <u>pe</u>cho	the chest
el <u>hom</u>bro	the shoulder
el pi<u>e</u>	the foot
el to<u>bi</u>llo	the ankle
la pi<u>er</u>na	the leg
la ro<u>di</u>lla	the knee
la ca<u>be</u>za	the head

la <u>len</u>gua	the tongue
la <u>bo</u>ca	the mouth
la es<u>pal</u>da	the back
la cin<u>tu</u>ra	the waist/the lower back
la cos<u>ti</u>lla	the rib
la <u>ma</u>no	the hand
la <u>u</u>ña	the nail

interrogatives

¿Qué es?   What is it?

conjunction

o   or

Es el brazo.

¿Es el brazo?   Sí, es el brazo.

¿Es el brazo?   Sí, _____.

Es el codo.

¿Es el codo?   Sí, _____.

Es el dedo.

¿Es el dedo?   Sí, _____.

¿Es el codo?   No, no es el _____.

¿Es el dedo?   No, no _____.

¿Qué es?   Es _____.

¿Qué es?   _____

¿Qué es?   _____

¿Qué ___?   Es el brazo.

____ __?   Es el codo.

____ __?   Es el dedo.

____ __ ?   Es el ojo.

____ __ ?   Es el labio.

____ __ ?   Es el cuello.

¿Es el ojo **o** es el cuello?   _____.

¿Es el cuello o es el labio?   _____.

¿Es el labio __ es el ojo?   _____.

____ __?   Es el estómago.

____ __ ?   Es el pecho.

____ __ ?   Es el hombro.

¿Es el hombro?   No, no es_____.

¿Qué es?   _____.

¿Es el pecho __ es el hombro?   _____.

¿Qué es?   _____.

____ ___?   Es el pie.

____ ___?   Es el tobillo.

¿Es el tobillo?   Sí, _____.

____ ___?   Es el pie.

Es la pierna.

¿Es la pierna?   Sí, _____.

¿Es la pierna?   No, _____.

_____ ___?   Es la rodilla

¿Es la pierna __ es la rodilla?   _____.

____ __?   Es la cabeza.

____ __?   Es la lengua.

____ __?   Es la boca.

¿Qué es?   _____.

¿Qué es?   _____.

¿Es la boca o es la lengua?   _____.

¿Es la lengua __ es la cabeza?   _____.

____ ___?   Es la espalda.

____ ___?   Es la cintura.

____ ___?   Es la costilla.

¿Es la cintura __ es la costilla?   _____.

¿Es la costilla __ es la espalda?   _____.

____ ___?   Es la mano.

Now wait just a minute. I was just getting the hang of it. **La** if it ends with **a**; **el** if it ends with **o**, and now you're telling me **la** man**o**? Must be a typo, right? Wrong. It's **la mano**... sorry.

____ __?   Es la uña.

¿Es la mano __ es la uña?   _____.

When you don't know the name of something in Spanish, you can always point and shrug your shoulders. But often pointing isn't enough (and sometimes, according to my mother, it's downright rude). So here's something with which you can accompany your pointing:

¿Qué es?   **What is it?**

Go around the room and point to everything you see and ask:
¿Qué es? ¿Qué es? ¿Qué es? You will never forget it (and neither will
anyone else sitting in the same room with you).

1.4 GENDER

The Spanish world view, being highly dualistic, separates the world of
objects into masculine and feminine. Surprisingly enough, it follows a
strange metaphysical logic rather than a sexist one (i.e., heart should be
feminine, but it's not; and force should be masculine, but it's not either).
The metaphisics can be boiled down to a somewhat consistent rule of
thumb:

If the ending vowel is **o**, the noun is **masculine**.
If the ending vowel is **a**, the noun is **feminine**.
If the ending vowel is **e**, you've got problems, the noun is either
masculine or feminine.

1.5 THE ARTICLE

In English, we have the democratic, all-objects-are-created-equal article
the. In Spanish, nouns are preceded by the definite article **el** if the noun is
masculine (ends with **o**), or by the definite article **la** if the noun is
feminine (ends with **a**). Indefinite articles, a finger, is **un dedo**; a
mouth, is **una boca**.

el brazo	la pierna
el codo	la rodilla
el ded_	la costill_
el hombr_	la cintur_
el cuell_	la boc_
_ pecho	_ lengua
_ estómago	_ man_ (just testing you)

There are exceptions, of course:
el agu**a** (the water)   **la** man**o** (the hand)
el problem**a** (the problem)   **la** radi**o** (guess)

1.6 THE PLURAL

Well, so much for sex. Now for numbers. Articles and nouns come in singular and plural.

el   ojo   **la**   pierna
los ojo**s**   **las** pierna**s**
el   labio   la   uña
____ labios   ____ uñas
el   tobillo   la   costilla

____ ____   la   mano

el   pie

____ ____   ____ ____

Note that as in English, to make a word plural, all you do is add an **s** to the end of the word.

Make the following articles and nouns plural:

el brazo   _____.
la boca   _____.
el pecho   _____.
la cabeza   _____.
el cuello   _____.
la espalda   _____.

1.7 WHO?

VOCABULARY AND STRESS GUIDE

nouns
la secretaria   the secretary
la enfermera   the nurse, f
el presidente   the president
los Estados Unidos   the United States
el primer ministro   the prime minister
la Inglaterra   England
el autor   the author

verbs
yo soy   I am

interrogatives
¿Quién es?   Who is?

Ana es la profesora.
¿Es Ana la profesora?   Sí, _____.
¿Es Ana la secretaria?   No, Ana no es ___.
¿Es Ana la paciente?   No, _____.
¿Es Ana la enfermera?   No, _____.

¿Quién es Ana?   Ana _____.
¿Quién es el presidente de los
  Estados Unidos?   _____.
_____ __ el primer ministro   de
  Inglaterra?   _____.
_____ _ el autor de *King Lear* ? _____.
_____ _ el autor de *El Quijote* ? _____.

Estudiante: ¿Es usted la secretaria?
Ana: No, yo no soy la secretaria.
Estudiante: ¿Quién es usted?
Ana: **Yo soy** la profesora.

Ana: ¿Es usted el paciente?
Estudiante: No, yo no _____.
Ana: ¿Es usted el presidente de los Estados
                                     Unidos?
Estudiante: No, _____.
Ana: ¿Es usted el autor de *Cien Años de
                                     Soledad* ?
Estudiante: No, _____.
Ana: ¿Quién es usted?
Estudiante: _____.

When you're pointing at a **thing**, you can say **¿qué es? (what is it?)** but
when you're pointing at a **person**, you have to say **¿quién es usted?
(who are you?)**. Now, go around the room and point to people, asking
¿quién es usted? ¿quién es usted? ¿quién es usted? Do this 50
times or until they lock you up.

1.8 THE PERSONAL PRONOUN

VOCABULARY AND STRESS GUIDE

nouns
el enfer<u>me</u>ro   the nurse, m

titles
Se<u>ñor</u>   Mister
Seño<u>ri</u>ta   Miss

verbs
yo soy   I am
us<u>ted</u> es   you are (formal)
él es   he is
<u>e</u>lla es   she is

Ramón es el padre.   **Él** es el padre.
Juancito es el niño.   ___ es el niño.
Señor Gómez es el paciente.   ___ es el paciente.

Rosa es la madre.   **Ella** es la madre.
Inéz es la niña.   ___ es la niña.
Señorita Díaz es la paciente.   ___ es la paciente.

1.8.1 The Verb "To Be"

yo soy   el doctor
                                                    la doctora
                                                    el enfermero
                                                    la enfermera

usted es   el paciente
                                                    la paciente

él es   el padre
                                                    el niño

ella es   la madre
                                                    la niña

In Spanish, the personal pronouns **yo (I), usted (you), él (he),** and **ella (she)** are often dropped. Later, you'll learn that this is because in Spanish, every person has its own verb-ending (it's own verb-what??). For now, I encourage you to use the pronouns and to point so there can be no misunderstanding as to whom you are referring.

If you've had any Spanish before, you've probably noticed that I'm just teaching you the formal way of addressing a person: **usted.** Use this form with elders, strangers, and anyone whom you would address as Mr., Mrs., or Miss in English. We only learn the formal in the <u>Manual</u> (it costs extra to learn the informal, but you can find the conjugations for the informal **tú** in the Appendix).

1.9 FORMATION OF THE POSSESSIVE

VOCABULARY AND STRESS GUIDE

nouns

el <u>va</u>so	the glass
el <u>ag</u>ua	the water
el <u>vin</u>o	the wine
la pediatría	pediatrics
la medi<u>ci</u>na	(the) medicine
la fa<u>mi</u>lia	the family

prepositions

de   o f

The Spanish temperament, not particularly concerned with compulsive time saving, never invented the "apostrophe s" (i.e., the mother**'s** arm); consequently, we have to do it the long way: the arm of the mother.

El brazo **de** la madre.   El vaso __ agua.
El niño __ la madre.   __ ___ __ vino.
La niña __ _____
If you want to say: the doctor of pediatrics, you'd say,

_____ __ _____

The student of medicine.

_____ __ _____

The student of medicine of the family.

_____ __ _____ __ __ _____

If you've got nothing better to do, memorize this:

de + el = del   **de + la = de la**

For example:

La niña **del** padre (el padre)   El niño **de la** madre (la madre)
El brazo _____ doctor (el doctor)   La uña __ __ enfermera (la
                                          enfermera)

1.10 PUTTING IT ALL TOGETHER

VOCABULARY AND STRESS GUIDE

nouns
el color   the color
el sombrero   the hat
la orina   the urine
el excremento   the excrement, stool
el esputo   the sputum
la sangre   the blood

adjectives
blanco/a   white
negro/a   black
rojo/a   red
amarillo/a   yellow
marrón   brown
verde   green
azul   blue

The glass **of** water   El vaso ___ agua
What is this?   ___ es?
Color   _____ (Invent!!!)
The hat **is** big   El sombrero __ grande

The urine (this you would
   have to look up in a diction-
   ary and come up with:)   la orina

Build:
Of what color is the urine?[1]   _ __ __ _ _ ____?

Translate the following into Spanish:
Of what color is the wine?   _____.
The wine is white.   _____ blanco.
Of what color is the eye?   _____.
The eye is black.   _____ negro.
Of what color is the blood?   _____.
The blood is red.   _____ roja.
Of what color is the urine?   _____.
The urine is yellow.   _____ amarilla.
Of what color is the excrement
  of the mother?   _____.
The excrement of the mother
  is brown.   _____ marrón.
Of what color is the sputum
  of the father?   _____.
The sputum of the father is green.   _____ verde.
Of what color is the eye of the girl?   _____.
The eye of the girl is blue.   _____ azul.

1.11 KEY CONCEPTS

Actually, out of the entire Lesson 1, I only want you to remember the following:

Me llamo   **¿Cómo se llama usted?**
Never pronounce "h"   **¿Qué es?**
¿De qué color es la orina? **¿Quién es?**

---

[1]Note that in Spanish, when speaking of something obviously belonging to the person (urine, excrement, or part of the body), we do not use the possessive pronoun "mine," "your," "his," or "hers." Instead we keep the definite article "the," **el** or **la.**

Lesson 1

La clínica de la medicina de la familia
(The Family Practice Clinic)

(You are the student speaking with the patient's mother, Señora Gómez.
Translate all the English into Spanish in the lines provided below).

Student: Good day. My name is Dr./   _____.
  Nurse/_____, I am the doctor/   _____.
  nurse/student of family medicine.   _____.
  What's your name?   _____.
Señora Gómez: Me llamo Señora Gómez.
Student: Who are you?   _____.
Señora Gómez: Yo soy la madre de Juancito.
Student: Who is Juancito?   _____.
Señora Gómez: Juancito es el paciente.
Student: Of what color is the
  urine of Juancito?   _____.
Señora Gómez: La orina es roja.
Student: Oh! Of what color is the
  excrement of Juancito?   _____.
Señora Gómez: El excremento es negro.
Student: Oh!   _____.

Translation
Student: Buenos días. Me llamo doctor/doctora/enfermero/enfermera/
  estudiante _____, soy el doctor/la doctora/el enfermero/la enfermera
  el estudiante de la medicina de la familia. ¿Cómo se llama usted?
Señora Gómez: My name is Mrs. Gómez.
Student: ¿Quién es usted?
Señora Gómez: I am the mother of Juancito.
Student: ¿Quién es Juancito?
Señora Gómez: Juancito is the patient.
Student: ¿De qué color es la orina de Juancito?
Señora Gómez: The urine is red.
Student: ¡Ah! ¿De qué color es el excremento de Juancito?
Señora Gómez: The stool is black.
Student: ¡Ah!

Now, go back to page 4 and look at the "Herpes" paragraph again. How much more can you
understand? (What! After all this work you still only understand "Herpes"?)

Lesson 2. Adjectives

2.1 WHAT IS IT LIKE?

VOCABULARY AND STRESS GUIDE

nouns

el lápiz	the pencil
el termómetro	the thermometer
la venda	the bandage
la nariz	the nose
el sombrero	the hat
la casa	the house

adjectives

corto/a	short (in length)
largo/a	long
grande	big
pequeño/a	small
mediano/a	medium
gordo/a	fat
bajo/a	short (in stature)
flaco/a	thin
alto/a	tall

interrogatives

¿Cómo es?	What is it like?

conjunction

y	and

title

Señora	Mrs.

El lápiz de Pepe es corto.

¿Es corto el lápiz de Pepe?   Sí, _____.

¿Es corto el termómetro ?   Sí, _____.

¿Es corto el lápiz de Juan?   No, el lápiz de Juan no es corto, el
                                      lápiz de Juan es **largo**.

¿Es largo el lápiz de Juan?   Sí, el lápiz de Juan es _____.

¿Es corto o es largo el lápiz
de Juan?   _____.

¿Es largo el lápiz de Pepe?   _____.

¿Cómo es el lápiz de Pepe?   _____.

¿Cómo es el lápiz de Juan?   _____.

_____ __ el lápiz de Pepe?   El lápiz de Pepe es corto.

_____ __ el lápiz de Juan?   El lápiz de Juan es largo.

_____ __ la pierna de Pepe?   La pierna de Pepe es corta.

_____ __ la venda?   La venda es larga.

_____ __ la nariz de Pinoquio?   _____.

El hospital es grande.

¿Es grande el hospital?   Sí, _____.

¿Es grande Tejas?   Sí, _____.

¿Es grande Delaware?   No, Delaware no es grande, Delaware
                                      es pequeño.

¿Cómo es Tejas?   _____.

_____ __ Delaware?   _____.

_____ __ el hospital?   _____.

La nariz de Thumbellina es pequeña, la nariz del[1] Señor Gómez es grande, **y**
  la nariz de la Señorita Arias es mediana.

---

[1]In Spanish, we put the definite article **el** or **la** in front of proper names preceded by a title. For
example:

El Señor Gómez es estudiante de medicina.

El presidente Bush es americano.

La Señora López es una enfermera.

La doctora Hernández no es americana.

La Señorita Arias no es una doctora.

Of note, many Hispanic males retain both their father's and mother's surnames in their own last
name, i.e., Señor Juan López Méndez (López is the father's surname, Méndez, the mother's
surname). The correct way to address him is either as Señor López or Señor López Méndez. His
wife would be Señora López or Señora de López.

¿Cómo es la nariz de Thumbellina?   _____.

____ __ la nariz del Señor Gómez?   _____.

____ __ la nariz de la
   Señorita Arias?   _____.

Pepe es gordo.

¿Es Pepe gordo?   Sí, _____.

¿Es Laurel (of "Laurel &
   Hardy") gordo?   Sí, _____.

Pepe es bajo.

¿Es Pepe bajo?   Sí, _____.

¿Es Pepe gordo y bajo?   _____.

Wait just a minute! **Pepe es bajo y no Pepe es corto**? That's right. **Bajo** means short in stature, and **corto** means short in length. Hard to believe, huh?

Juan es flaco.

¿Es Juan flaco?   Sí, _____.

¿Es Hardy flaco?   Sí, _____.

Juan es alto.

¿Es Juan alto?   Sí, _____.

¿Es Juan flaco y alto?   _____.

What if in English we didn't say, "What is Pepe like?" but said, "What is like Pepe?" or, taking it a step further, if we said, **¿Cómo es Pepe?** Life would be so easy then, because that's exactly how we say it in Spanish!

¿Es Pepe flaco?   No, Pepe no _____

¿Es Pepe alto?   No, Pepe _____

¿Cómo es Pepe?   Pepe es ____ y ____

¿Cómo es Juan?   Juan es ____ y ____

¿Cómo es Laurel?   Laurel es _____

¿Cómo es Hardy?   Hardy es _____

____ __ Pepe?   Pepe es gordo.

____ __ Juan?   Juan es flaco.

_____ __ la madre del paciente?   La madre del paciente es gorda.
_____ __ el padre del niño?   El padre del niño es alto.

2.2 ADJECTIVES

By now you've probably noticed that the adjectives agree in gender with
the noun. (If you haven't, aren't you glad I brought it up?) Masculine nouns
end in **o** and their adjectives also end in **o**:

El termómetro es cort**o**
El brazo es cort_
El cuello es larg_
El dedo es pequeñ_

Feminine nouns end in **a** and their adjectives also end in **a**:

La uña es cort**a**
La pierna es cort_
La costilla es larg_
La cintura es pequeñ_

But... but... I know, but what about **el cuarto es grande**? or **la cabeza es
grande**? O.K. I'm not perfect, and neither is Spanish. Adjectives that end
in **e** always end in **e**, whether the noun they modify is masculine or
feminine.

2.3 SYNTAX

In Spanish, the syntax (the word order in a sentence, for those of you who
think this is something located between the larynx and the pharynx) is
very similar to English.

subject	verb	adjective
the hospital	is	big
el hospital	es	grande

(See how simple Spanish is?)

I know that I'm not supposed to encourage you to translate word for word (that teaching method went out before Socrates, I think), but often, you can translate *verbatim* (this is Latin), keeping the same order and logic in declarative sentences (this is English). This is a good trick when you're inventing, which I henceforth encourage you to do.

2.4 INTERROGATIVES

The syntax changes slightly in a question, by reversing the order of the subject and the verb, as in English:

verb	subject	adjective
Is	the hospital	big?
¿Es	el hospital	grande?

The correct way of asking this question is indicated in the exercises: **¿es grande el hospital?** But you can get away with saying: **¿es el hospital grande?** and keeping the exact English construction, if it helps.

Later on, you'll learn that in Spanish, **there is no such thing as "do?" "does?" or "did?"** (If you don't learn it later, you might as well learn it now: **In Spanish, there is no such thing as "do?" "does?" or "did?"**) Do you get the feeling that this is kind of important?

If you forget how to ask a question, don't panic. Merely turn your statement into a question by inflecting your voice (adding a question mark at the end of the declarative sentence) and **raising your eyebrows.**

Are you the mother?	¿Es usted _____?
Are you the patient?	_____?
Are you the mother of the patient?	_____?

Is she the mother?	¿Es ella _____?
Is he the boy?	_____?
Is she the mother of the boy?	_____?

In Spanish, we nestle the question in question marks, and the opening question mark is inverted. Same for exclamation marks.

2.5 NEGATION

To negate a sentence in English, we put the "not" **after** the verb: "Ana's nose **is not** long." In Spanish, we put the "no" **before** the verb: "La nariz de Ana **no es** larga."

La nariz de Pinoquio **no** es corta.
La nariz de Ana __ es larga.
El hospital __ es pequeño.
El presidente Bush __ es mejicano.
_____ (the hat of Juan not is small)

2.6 BUT

¿Es Pepe gordo?   Sí, Pepe es gordo.
¿Es Pepe gordo y flaco?   No, Pepe es gordo **pero no** es flaco.
¿Es Pepe gordo y alto?   No, Pepe es _____ pero **no** es alto.

¿Es Pepe bajo?   Sí, _____.
¿Es Pepe bajo y flaco?   No, Pepe es bajo _____ **no** es flaco.

¿Es Juan flaco y bajo?   No, Juan es flaco _____.
¿Es Juan alto y gordo?   No, Juan es alto _____.
¿Es Laurel gordo y alto?   No, Laurel es gordo _____.
¿Es la nariz de Pinoquio larga?   Sí, _____.
¿Es la nariz de Pinoquio larga
   y verde?   No, _____.

2.7 COMPARISONS

Pepe es **más gordo que** Juan.
Pepe es ___ gordo ___ Juan.
Pepe es ___ bajo ___ Juan.
Juan es ___ flaco ___ Pepe.
Juan es ___ alto ___ Pepe.

¿Quién es más gordo, Pepe o Juan?   _____.
¿Quién es más flaco, Pepe o Juan?   _____.

Juan es **menos gordo que** Pepe.
Juan es _____ gordo __ Pepe.
Juan es _____ bajo __ Pepe.
Pepe es _____ flaco __ Juan.
Pepe es _____ alto __ Juan.

¿Quién es menos gordo, Pepe o Juan? _____.
¿Quién es menos alto, Pepe o Juan?   _____.

México es ___ grande __ Nicaragua.
La nariz de Pinoquio es ___ larga ___ la nariz de Ana.
El dedo es ___ corto ___ la pierna.

This is one case when you can't invent. Gordoer does not exist! To say "fatter than" in Spanish, we have to do it the long way around:

more fat than   **más gordo que**

less thin than   **menos flaco que**

All comparisons work this way:

_____ big   _____ bigger than
_____ tall   _____ taller than
_____ big   _____ less big than
_____ yellow   _____ less yellow than

2.8 WHICH?

VOCABULARY AND STRESS GUIDE

nouns
un país   a country

adjectives
hispano   hispanic
quebrado   broken
cortado   cut
quemado   burnt
hinchado   swollen

infec<u>ta</u>do   infected
infla<u>ma</u>do   inflamed

interrogatives
¿cuál?   which?

¿Es grande El Salvador?   No, _____.
¿Es grande Liechtenstein?   No, _____.
¿Es grande Cuba?   No, _____.
¿Cuál es un país grande?   Rusia _____.
¿Cuál es un país pequeño?   Inglaterra _____.
_____ es un país hispano?   Guatemala _____.
_____ es un país hispano y grande? Argentina _____.

Translate into Spanish:
Which is the finger of Pepe?   _____.
Which is the finger broken?   _____**dedo quebrado**?
Which is the finger broken of Pepe? _____.
Which is the ankle broken?   _____.
Which is the elbow broken?   _____.

Which is the arm of Juan?   _____.
Which is the arm cut?   _____**brazo cortado**?
Which is the arm cut of Juan?   _____.
Which is the shoulder cut?   _____.
Which is the nail cut?   _____cort**ada**?

Which is the foot of Pepe?   _____.
Which is the foot burnt?   _____**pie quemado**?
Which is the foot burnt of Pepe?   _____.
Which is the leg burnt?   _____.
Which is the knee burnt?   _____.

Which is the eye of Juan?   _____.
Which is the eye swollen?   _____**ojo hinchado**?
Which is the eye swollen of Juan? _____.
Which is the hand swollen?   _____.
Which is the ankle swollen?   _____.

Which is the finger infected?   _____.
Which is the finger inflamed?   _____.

2.9 ADJECTIVAL ORDER

VOCABULARY AND STRESS GUIDE

nouns

el l<u>ib</u>ro	the book
la infección	the infection
el cu<u>a</u>rto	the room

adjectives

p<u>ú</u>blico/a	public
priv<u>a</u>do/a	private
<u>se</u>rio/a	serious

What do you mean, the finger infected, the leg burnt? I mean that in Spanish, we always put the **noun first**, the **adjective second**, which is the reverse of English. In English, one sees the white before the horse (the white horse), while in Spanish, we see the horse first, and then the fact that it's white (el caballo blanco).

La pierna larga	The leg long
El libro grande	The book big
_____	The finger short
_____	The finger swollen
_____	The arm long
_____	The arm cut
_____	The hospital big
_____	The hospital public
_____	The room private
_____	The infection red
_____	The infection serious
_____	The mother serious

2.10 POSSESSIVE PRONOUNS

Juan: ¡Es **mi** venda, **mi** libro, y **mi** lápiz!
Pepe: ¡No! ¡Es **mi** venda, **mi** libro, y **mi** lápiz!
Juan: ¡Es **mi** venda!

Pepe: No Juan, no es **su** venda, ¡es **mi** venda!
Juan: ¡No Pepe! No es __ venda, ¡es ___ venda!
Pepe: ¡Es **mi** libro!
Juan: ¡No Pepe! No es __ libro, ¡es ___ libro!
Pepe: ¡Es **mi** lápiz!
Juan: ¡No Pepe! No es ___ lápiz, ¡es ___ lápiz!

Ana: Pepe, ¿es **su** lápiz?
Pepe: Sí, es **mi** lápiz.
Juan: No, Ana, no es **su** lápiz, ¡es **mi** lápiz!
Ana: Juan, ¿es **su** venda?
Juan: Sí, es ___ venda.
Pepe: No, Ana, no es ___ venda, ¡es ___ venda!
Ana: Pepe, ¿es **su** libro?
Pepe: Sí, es ___ libro.
Juan: No, Ana, no es ___ libro, ¡es ___ libro!

I guess I better explain myself before Pepe and Juan get into a fight or you throw this libro out the window. Actually, it is much easier than you think. In Spanish,

your book ⎫
 his book ⎬   is simply-----> **su libro**
her book ⎪
 its book ⎭

your head ⎫
 his head ⎬   is simply-----> **su cabeza**
her head ⎪
 its head ⎭

Sometimes, to avoid confusion (we say it in English... just kidding), we say:

your book   **el libro <u>de</u> usted**
his book   **el libro <u>de</u> él**[2]
her book   **el libro <u>de</u> ella**

_____

[2]de + el señor = del señor
 de + él (he) = de él

your head	**la cabeza <u>de</u> usted**
his head	**la cabeza <u>de</u> él**
her head	**la cabeza <u>de</u> ella**

2.11 WHOSE?

VOCABULARY AND STRESS GUIDE

nouns

el café   the coffee

Do you remember how to say:

___ es el presidente de los Estados Unidos?
(**Who** is the president of the United States?)

Then build:

Of who(m) is the urine?
_____?

_____?   _____?
                                   Of whom is the boy? (Whose boy is it?)
_____?   Of whom is the pencil white? (Whose
                                       white pencil is it?)
_____?   Of whom is the coffee?
_____?   Of whom is the coffee black?
_____?   Of whom is the pencil?

2.12 EXPRESSIONS

VOCABULARY AND STRESS GUIDE

nouns
la aspi<u>ri</u>n a   the aspirin

adjectives
<u>do</u>ble   double

verbs

Yo quiero	I want
¿Quiere usted?	Do you want?

expressions

por favor	please
gracias	thank you

Yo quiero un cuarto privado, por favor.
Yo quiero _____ doble, _____
_____   el doctor,   _____
_____   la enfermera,   _____

¿Quiere usted un cuarto privado?
¿Quiere usted _____ doble?
_____ _____ una aspirina?
Sí, gracias, quiero una aspirina.
Sí, _____ , quiero un cuarto privado.

Translate into Spanish:
I want a glass of water, please.   _____.
I do not want the doctor, please.   _____.
Yes, I want a glass of water
  and an aspirin, please.   _____.
Yes, thank you, I want a
  private room.   _____.
Do you want the doctor or
  the nurse?   _____.
What do you want?   _____.
Whom do you want?   _____.

whew!!!!

2.13 KEY CONCEPTS

¿Cómo es Pepe?	What is Pepe like?
Pepe es más gordo que Juan	Pepe is fatter than Juan
¿Cuál es el dedo infectado?	Which is the infected finger?
¿Es su orina?	Is this your urine?

Lesson 2

La sala de emergencia: El trauma
(The Emergency Room: Trauma)

(translate this out loud)   **(check yourself with this)**

Good day! I call myself_____   Buenos días. Me llamo _____
I am the doctor/nurse/medical   Yo soy el(la)doctor(a)/el(la) enfer-
  student.   mero(a)/el(la) estudiante de
                                           medicina.

How do you call yourself?   ¿Cómo se llama usted?

Who is he?   ¿Quién es él?
Are you the mother?   ¿Es usted la madre?
Are you the mother of the boy?   ¿Es usted la madre del niño?
How does the boy call himself?   ¿Cómo se llama el niño?

What is the problem?   ¿Qué es el problema?
What is this? (looking at the finger)   ¿Qué es?
Which is the broken finger?   ¿Cuál es el dedo quebrado?
Which is the cut arm?   ¿Cuál es el brazo cortado?
Which is the swollen eye?   ¿Cuál es el ojo hinchado?
Which is the burnt leg?   ¿Cuál es la pierna quemada?

Of what color is the urine   ¿De qué color es la
  of your boy?   orina de su niño?
I want the broken finger of   Quiero el dedo quebrado del niñõ,
  the boy. Thank you.   por favor. Gracias.

This is the bandage.   Es la venda.
This is the long bandage.   Es la venda larga.
The swollen eye is not serious.   El ojo hinchado no es serio.
The cut arm is not serious.   El brazo cortado no es serio.
The broken finger is not serious.   El dedo quebrado no es serio.
But the burnt leg is serious.   Pero la pierna quemada es seria.

What do you want?   ¿Qué quiere?
The boy wants a glass of water.   El niño quiere un vaso de agua.
The boy wants his father.   El niño quiere su padre.

The mother of the boy
  wants aspirin.
No, not aspirin, Tylenol. Good bye.
	La madre del niño
	  quiere aspirina.
	No, aspirina no.Tylenol, sí. Adiós.

Now, go back to page 4 and look at the "Herpes" paragraph again. How much more can you understand?

Lesson 3. The Verb "To Be"

3.1 TO BE IN A PERMANENT WAY (SER)

3.1.1 My Family Tree

VOCABULARY AND STRESS GUIDE

nouns

el esp<u>o</u>so	the husband
la esp<u>o</u>sa	the wife
el h<u>ij</u>o	the son
la h<u>ij</u>a	the daughter
el her<u>ma</u>no	the brother
la her<u>ma</u>na	the sister
el tío	the uncle
la tía	the aunt
la <u>pri</u>ma	the cousin, f
el <u>pri</u>mo	the cousin, m
la abu<u>e</u>la	the grandmother
el abu<u>e</u>lo	the grandfather

adjectives

del<u>ga</u>do/a	slim
o<u>be</u>so/a	obese
vi<u>e</u>jo/a	old
<u>jo</u>ven	young
ma<u>yor</u>	older
me<u>nor</u>	younger

Study the family tree below. No, this book is not suddenly turning into a Russian novel (although I'm sure you've been suspicious for a while now). Pretend that you are taking a family history from your Spanish-speaking patient, Ana, and want to know what each family member is like (something you would never do in real life, of course.)

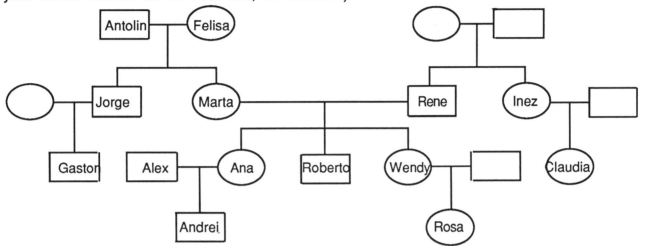

Usted

¿Cómo se llama su madre?

¿Cómo es su madre?

_____?

¿Cómo es su _____?

¿Cómo se llama su esposo ?

_____?

_____?

_____?

¿Cómo se llama su hermano?

_____?

¿Cómo se llama su hermana?

_____?

_____?

_____?

¿Cómo se llama su tío?

_____?

¿Cómo se llama su tía?

_____?

¿Cómo se llama su prima?

_____?

¿Cómo se llama su primo?

_____?

¿Cómo se llama su abuela?

Ana

_____ Marta.

Mi madre es gorda.

Mi padre se llama René.

Mi padre es flaco.

_____ Alex.

Mi esposo es alto y flaco.

Mi hijo se llama Andrei.

Mi hijo es pequeño.

_____ se llama Roberto.

Mi hermano es delgado.

_____ se llama Wendy.

Mi hermana es delgada.

La hija de mi hermana se llama Rosa.

La hija de mi hermana es pequeña.

_____ se llama Jorge.

Mi tío Jorge no es obeso.

_____ se llama Inez.

Mi tía Inez no es obesa.

_____ se llama Claudia.

Mi prima Claudia es flaca.

_____ se llama Gastón.

Mi primo Gastón es flaco.

_____ se llama Felisa.

_____?   Mi abuela es vieja.
¿Cómo se llama su abuelo?   _____ se llama Antolín.
_____?   Mi abuelo es viejo.
_____?   Andrei es joven.
¿Cómo es su abuela?
¿Cómo es su hijo?   _____.
¿Es su abuela mayor que su madre?   _____.
¿Es su abuelo mayor que su padre?   Sí, mi abuela es _____ mi madre.
_____?   Sí, _____.
                                               Sí, mi tío Jorge es mayor que mi
¿Es su hijo Andrei menor   primo Gastón.
   que Roberto?
¿Es su madre menor que   Sí, Andrei es _____ Roberto.
   su padre?
_____?   Sí, _____.
                                               Sí, Wendy es menor que yo.

3.1.2 My Furniture

VOCABULARY AND STRESS GUIDE

nouns
la cama   the bed

adjectives
cómodo/a   comfortable
incómodo/a   uncomfortable
blando/a   soft
duro/a   hard
derecho/a   right
izquierdo/a   left

¿Qué es?
Es la cama de mi hijo Andrei.
La cama de mi hijo Andrei es pequeña.
¿Es grande o es pequeña la cama de
   Andrei?   _____.

La cama de Andrei es cómoda.
¿Cómo es la cama de Andrei?   _____ es cómoda.
¿Es cómoda la cama de Andrei?   Sí, _____.

Mi cama es incómoda.
¿Cómo es mi cama?   Su _____.
¿Es cómoda o es incómoda mi cama?   _____.

La cama de Andrei es blanda.
¿Cómo es la cama de Andrei?   _____ es blanda.
¿Es dura o es blanda la cama de
   Andrei?   _____.

Mi cama es dura.
¿Cómo es mi cama?   Su _____.
¿Es blanda o es dura mi cama?   _____.

La cama derecha es grande.
La cama izquierda es pequeña.
¿Es grande la cama derecha?   Sí, _____ es grande.
¿Cómo es la cama derecha?   _____.

¿Es pequeña la cama izquierda?   Sí, _____ es pequeña.
¿Cómo es la cama izquierda?   _____.

3.1.3 Cuts and Bruises

VOCABULARY AND STRESS GUIDE

nouns

el tajo	the cut
el dolor	the pain

adjectives

profundo/a	deep
temporario/a	temporary
permanente	permanent
repentino/a	sudden
gradual	gradual
severo/a	severe
local	local
general	generalized

adverbs

progresiva<u>mente</u>   progressively

¿Qué es?

Es el tajo.

El tajo en el brazo izquierdo es superficial.

¿Es superficial el tajo en
   el brazo izquierdo?   Sí, _____.

¿Cómo es el tajo en
   el brazo izquierdo?   _____.

El tajo en el brazo derecho es profundo.

¿Es profundo el tajo en
   el brazo derecho?   Sí, _____.

¿Es superficial o es profundo
   el tajo en el brazo derecho?   _____.

¿Cómo es el tajo en el brazo
   derecho?   _____.

El dolor en el brazo izquierdo es superficial.

¿Es el dolor en el brazo izquierdo
   superficial?   Sí, _____.

¿Cómo es el dolor en
   el brazo izquierdo?   El dolor en el brazo izquierdo
                                           es _____.

_____ __ el dolor en
   el brazo derecho?   El dolor en el brazo derecho es
                                           profundo.

_____ __ el dolor?   El dolor es temporario.

_____ __ _____ ?   El dolor es permanente.

_____ __ _____ ?   El dolor es repentino.

_____ __ _____ ?   El dolor es gradual.

_____ __ _____ ?   El dolor es severo.

_____ __ _____ ?   El dolor es local.

_____ __ _____ ?   El dolor es general.

_____ __ _____ ?   El dolor es progresivamente...

Translate into Spanish:

The pain is progressively
   more severe.   _____.

What's the pain like?   _____.

3.2 TO BE IN A TEMPORARY WAY

VOCABULARY AND STRESS GUIDE

nouns

la ca<u>mi</u>sa	the shirt
la <u>fren</u>te	the forehead
el café	the coffee
el té	the tea
el líquido	the liquid
la tempera<u>tu</u>ra	the temperature
la presión	the blood pressure
el <u>pul</u>so	the pulse

adjectives

mo<u>ja</u>do/a	wet
<u>se</u>co/a	dry
<u>su</u>cio/a	dirty
<u>lim</u>pio/a	clean
cali<u>e</u>nte	hot
frío/a	cold
en<u>fer</u>mo/a	ill
<u>sa</u>no/a	healthy
embara<u>za</u>da	pregnant
pálido/a	pale
resfri<u>a</u>do/a	sick with a cold
nervi<u>o</u>so/a	nervous
inconci<u>e</u>nte	unconscious
nor<u>mal</u>	normal

verbs

yo es<u>toy</u>	I am
us<u>ted</u> está	you are

interrogatives

¿Cómo está ...?	How is ....?

Andrei está mojado.
La mano de Andrei está mojada.
¿Cómo está la mano de Andrei?   La mano _____.

Rosa está seca.
La mano de Rosa está seca.
¿Cómo está la mano de Rosa?   La mano _____.

Roberto está sucio.
La pierna de Roberto está sucia.
¿Cómo está la pierna de Roberto?   La pierna _____.

Marta está limpia.
La pierna de Marta está limpia.
¿Cómo está la pierna de Marta?   La pierna _____.

¿Cómo ____ la pierna de Marta?   La pierna de Marta está limpia.
____ ____ la frente de Andrei?   La frente de Andrei está ____.
____ ____ la camisa de Andrei?   La camisa _____.
____ ____ el café?   El café está caliente.
____ ____ el té?   El té _____.
____ ____ el agua?   El agua _____ fría.[1]
____ ____ el líquido?   El líquido _____.
____ ____ Wendy?   Wendy ____ enferma.
____ ____ el esposo de Wendy?   El esposo de Wendy no está
                                             enfermo, él ____ sano.

____ ____ Claudia?   Claudia ____ embarazada.

¿Está Wendy sana?   No, Wendy no _____.
¿Cómo está Wendy?   Wendy está _____.
¿Cómo está el esposo de Wendy?   El esposo de Wendy _____.
¿Cómo está Claudia?   Claudia _____.

____ ____ Gastón?   Gastón está pálido.
____ ____ Alex?   Alex está resfriado.
____ ____ la madre de Alex?   La madre de Alex está nerviosa.

¿Está Gastón resfriado?   No, Gastón no _____.
¿Está Gastón nervioso?   No, _____.
¿Cómo está Gastón?   Gastón está _____.
¿Cómo está Alex?   Alex _____.
¿Cómo está la madre de Alex?   La madre de Alex _____.

---

[1]**El agua** is really a feminine word with a masculine article so the adjective, which always agrees in gender with the noun it modifies, is feminine, *ergo*: **el agua fría.**

_____ _____ el paciente?	El paciente está inconciente.
_____ _____ Claudia?	Claudia está embarazada.
_____ _____ Ana?	Ana está normal.

¿Está el paciente nervioso?	No, el paciente no _____.
¿Está el paciente normal?	No, _____.
¿Cómo está el paciente?	El paciente está _____.
¿Cómo está Claudia?	Claudia _____.
¿Cómo está Ana?	Ana _____.

¿Cómo está la temperatura?	_____ está alta.
_____ ___ la presión?	_____ baja.
_____ ___ el pulso?	_____ alto.

¿Cómo está usted?	Yo estoy sana.
¿Cómo está usted?	Yo ___ resfriada/o.
¿Cómo está usted?	___ estoy nerviosa/o.
¿Cómo está usted?	_____ enferma/o.
_____?	Yo estoy pálida/o.
_____?	Yo estoy bien.
_____?	Yo estoy mal.

3.3 TO BE IN A PLACE

VOCABULARY AND STRESS GUIDE

nouns

la casa	the house
el ombligo	the navel
la fractura	the fracture

adverbs

aquí	here

El paciente **está** en el cuarto.
El cuarto **está** en el hospital.
El hospital **está** en San Francisco.
San Francisco **está** en California.
California **está** en los Estados Unidos.

¿Está el paciente en Hawaii?   No, el paciente **no está** en_____.
¿Está el paciente en Acapulco?   No, _____.
¿Está el paciente en Tahiti?   No, _____.
¿Dónde está el paciente?   El paciente está en _____.
¿Dónde está el cuarto?   _____.
¿Dónde está el hospital?   _____.
¿Dónde está San Francisco?   _____.
¿Dónde está California?   _____.
____ ___ su casa?   _____.
____ ___ su madre?   Mi madre está en El Salvador.
____ ___ su padre?   Mi padre está en Guatemala.
____ ___ su ____?   Mi familia está en Centro America.
____ ___ el dolor?   El dolor ____ en el estómago.
____ ___ el dolor?   El dolor ____ en el ombligo.
_____?   El tajo está en el brazo derecho.
_____?   La fractura está en la pierna izquierda.
_____?   El dolor está aquí.
_____?   El tajo está aquí.
_____?   La fractura ___ ___ (is here).

Build:

Is here the fracture?
(Is the fracture here?)   _____?

Is here the pain?
(Is the pain here?)   _____?

Is here the cut?
(Is the cut here?)   _____?

¿Dónde está usted?   **Yo estoy** en el hospital.
¿Está usted en el hospital?   Sí, yo estoy _____.
¿Está usted en San Francisco?   _____.
¿Está usted en México?   _____.
¿Está usted en Arizona?   _____.
¿Dónde está usted?   _____.

3.4 A VERY CONFUSING VERB: TO BE

Now that you've retrieved the book from out the window, we can unravel the mess I've probably created in your poor, taxed brain. Have you gotten as far as to wonder why you say **¿cómo está?** sometimes, and **¿cómo es?** other times? (Good.)   Well, believe it or not, it's not arbitrary. But unfortunately, it's also not consistent. (Great.) Here goes:

3.4.1 ¿Cómo es? "To Be" in a Permanent Way

Ser (the infinitive of **es**) is the verb "to be" that we use before adjectives of **permanent or inherent characteristics.**   If you want to ask **what** anything or anybody **is like** (fat, skinny, obese, tall, short, comfortable, hard, soft, superficial, permanent, sudden, gradual, explosive, etc.), you say **¿cómo es?**

¿cómo es él?	means what is he like?
¿cómo es ella?	means what is she like?
¿cómo es?	means what is it like?
¿cómo es usted?	means what are you like?

3.4.2 ¿Cómo está? "To Be" in a Temporary Way

Estar (infinitive of **está**) is the verb "to be" that we use before adjectives that are **temporary**, that is, that can change from one instance to the next. So, if you want to ask **how** anything or anybody **is** (pale, sick, healthy, nervous, unconscious, wet, dry, clean, dirty, well, not well, pregnant, high or low [as in pulse, blood pressure, or temperature]), you say **¿cómo está?**

¿cómo está él?	means how is he?
¿cómo está ella?	means how is she?
¿cómo está?	means how is it?
¿cómo está usted?	means how are you?

3.4.3 ¿Dónde está? "To Be" in a Place

Estar (the infinitive of **está**) is the verb "to be" which we use when describing **location**. If you want to ask **where** anything or anybody **is** (here, in the hospital, in the head, in New York, in Guatemala, etc.), you say **¿dónde está?**

¿dónde está él?	means where is he?
¿dónde está ella?	means where is she?
¿dónde está?	means where is it?
¿dónde está usted?	means where are you?

3.4.4 The Not-So-Very-Confusing Verb "To Be"

Remembering that: **always-es, sometimes-está, and location-está**, translate the following:

The patient is sick (maybe he'll be
  well tomorrow, who knows)   _____.
The patient is tall (unlikely that
  he'll be short tomorrow)   _____.
The patient is here (location)   _____.

The foot is big (always).   _____.
The foot is dirty (usually, but
  not always).   _____.
The foot is in the mouth (location). _____.

If you can't remember most of what we just learned, don't fret, just mumble.

3.5 EXPRESSIONS

VOCABULARY AND STRESS GUIDE

nouns

el cirujano	the surgeon, m
la cirujana	the surgeon, f
la operación	the operation
el apéndice	the appendix

verbs

yo nece<u>si</u>to	I need
usted nece<u>si</u>ta	you need

adverbs

inmediata<u>men</u>te	immediately

Translate into Spanish:

I need the doctor.	Yo necesito _____.
I need the nurse.	_____.
I need the surgeon.	_____ el cirujano.
Do you need the doctor?	Necesita usted _____.
Do you need a glass of water?	_____.
Do you need the surgeon?	_____.
You need the doctor.	Usted necesita _____.
You need the operation.	_____ la operación.
You need the operation of the appendix.	_____ del apéndice.
You need the operation of the appendix immediately.	_____ inmediatamente.

3.6 KEY CONCEPTS

¿Dónde está el dolor?	Where is the pain?
¿Cómo es el dolor?	What is the pain like?
¿Cómo está usted?	How are you?
Usted necesita...	You need...

Lesson 3

La cirujía: El abdomen agudo
(Surgery: The Acute Abdomen)

(translate this out loud)   **(check yourself with this)**

(Speaking to the patient, a 10-year-old boy):

Good day. I call myself _____	Buenos días. Me llamo _____
How do you call yourself?	¿Cómo se llama usted?
I am the surgeon/surgery nurse.	Soy el cirujano/la cirujana/el(la) enfermero(a) de cirujía.
Where is your mother?	¿Dónde está su madre?
Here is your mother!	¡Aquí está su madre!

(Speaking now to the mother):

Is your son?	¿Es su hijo?
How do you call yourself?	¿Cómo se llama?
I call myself ___. I am the surgeon.	Me llamo ____ Soy el/la cirujano/a.
Is sick your son? (temporary)	¿Está enfermo su hijo?
Normally, your son is healthy? (permanent, inherent)	¿Normalmente, su hijo es sano?
Your son is pale, but he is not unconscious. (temporary)	Su hijo está pálido, pero no está inconciente.
His forehead is hot and wet.	Su frente está caliente y mojada.
Are you nervous? I'm sorry.	¿Está nerviosa? Lo siento.

(Speaking back to the son):

What is the pain like?	¿Cómo es el dolor?
Is the pain temporary or permanent?	¿Es el dolor temporario o permanente?
Deep or superficial? Gradual or sudden? Local or general?	¿Profundo o superficial? ¿Gradual o repentino? ¿Local o general?
Progressively more severe?	¿Progresivamente más severo?
Where is the pain?	¿Dónde está el dolor?
In the stomach? In the navel?	¿En el estómago? ¿En el ombligo?
Is the pain here more severe than here? Where is	¿Es el dolor aquí más severo que aquí? ¿Dónde está

the pain more severe?	el dolor más severo?
(Where is the worst pain?)	
Is the pain right more	¿Es el dolor derecho
severe than the pain left?	más severo que el dolor izquierdo?
What's like the excrement?	¿Cómo es el excremento?
Is like diarrhea?	¿Es como diarrea?
Of what color is the excrement?	¿De qué color es el excremento?
Red?	¿Rojo?
Of what color is the urine? Red?	¿De qué color es la orina? ¿Roja?
What's like the nausea? Is severe?	¿Cómo es la náusea? ¿Es severa?
What's like the vomit? Is severe?	¿Cómo es el vómito? ¿Es severo?

(back to the mother):

Mrs. ____, is appendicitis.	Señora ____, es apendicitis.
Appendicitis is an inflamation	Apendicitis es una inflamación
of the appendix. Is common	del apéndice. Es común
in children, but is serious.	en niños, pero es serio.
I am sorry but your son	Lo siento, pero su hijo
needs an operation immediately.	necesita una operación
	inmediatamente.

Now, go back to page 4 and look at the "Herpes" paragraph again. How much more can you understand?

Lesson 4. The Present

4.1 PREPOSITIONS

VOCABULARY AND STRESS GUIDE

nouns

la mesa	the table
la vejiga	the bladder
el útero	the uterus
la oreja	the ear
el cuerpo	the body
el riñón	the kidney

prepositions

encima de	on top of
debajo de	beneath of
delante de	in front of
detrás de	in back of
al lado de	to the side of
a la derecha de	to the right of
a la izquierda de	to the left of

El sombrero está **encima de** la cabeza.
El paciente está encima de la cama.
El vaso de agua está encima de la mesa.

¿Dónde está el sombrero? _____.
¿Dónde está el paciente? _____.
¿Dónde está el vaso de agua? _____.

La cabeza está **debajo del** sombrero.
La cama está debajo del paciente.
La mesa está debajo del vaso de agua.

¿Dónde está la cabeza?   _____.
¿Dónde está la cama?   _____.
¿Dónde está la mesa?   _____.

La nariz está **delante de** la cabeza.
La vejiga está delante del útero.
La rodilla está delante de la pierna.

¿Dónde está la nariz?   _____.
¿Dónde está la vejiga?   _____.
¿Dónde está la rodilla?   _____.

La cabeza está **detrás de** la nariz.
El útero está detrás de la vejiga.
La pierna está detrás de la rodilla.

¿Dónde está la cabeza?   _____.
¿Dónde está el útero?   _____.
¿Dónde está la pierna?   _____.

La oreja está **al lado de** la cabeza.
El brazo está al lado del cuerpo.
El riñón está al lado de la aorta.

¿Dónde está la oreja?   _____.
¿Dónde está el brazo?   _____.
¿Dónde está el riñón?   _____.

La oreja derecha está **a la derecha de** la cabeza.
La oreja izquierda está **a la izquierda** de la cabeza.

¿Está la oreja derecha a la derecha
   o a la izquierda de la cabeza?   _____.
¿Está la oreja izquierda a la derecha o a la izquierda de la cabeza? _____.

(Remember, the verb "to be" in these sentences is always used to indicate
location, therefore, we use **estar**.)

Translate into Spanish:

Is the pain above the navel?   _____ .

Is the pain below the uterus?   _____ .

Is the pain above or below
  the stomach?   _____ .

Is the pain to the right of
  my finger?   _____ .

Is the pain to the left of my finger? _____ .

The clinic is behind the hospital.   _____ .

The elevator is in front of
  the clinic. (Invent!)   _____ .

The pharmacy is next to
  the hospital. (Invent!)   _____ .

The emergency room is to
  the right of the elevator. Wow!!   _____ .

4.2 THE VERB

I think we're due for a little action. After all, here we are, on Lesson 4 and
we still haven't heard a word about verbs. Is she going to tell us that verbs
(outside of the two forms "to be") don't exist? That Spanish people talk in
nouns and adjectives only? Actually, only Spanish students talk that way,
Spanish speakers do use verbs. As a matter of fact, they use at least one in
every sentence.

4.2.1 Pronouns

In English, verbs are hardly conjugated (except for the 3rd person). For
example, the verb "to take" is conjugated, "I take, you take, we take, they
take ... " Not so in Spanish, where verbs are conjugated so that every person
gets its own verb-ending. (The exceptions are 2nd and 3rd person that take
the same endings.) Therefore, because the person is understood from the
verb-ending, the pronoun (I, you, he, she, it, we, and they, for those of you
who took grammar in the third grade with Mrs. Bostich, whom you never liked
anyway) is not necessary. Then why learn them you ask? Because if you get
the ending wrong you'll at least have the pronoun ... that is, assuming that you
know your pronouns.

yo	**I**
(tú)	**(you, inf., sing)**
usted	**you, form., sing.**
él	**he**
ella	**she**
	it[1]
nosotros	**we**
ustedes	**you, plural**
ellos	**they, masculine**
ellas	**they, feminine**

4.2.2 Verb Group Endings

There are three things to remember about verbs:

1. Verbs come **regular** and **irregular** (on sale for half price). The regular verbs are well behaved and follow conjugation rules without exceptions (see below). The irregular verbs break all the rules without exceptions. My advice is to forget about the irregular verbs, learn the endings to the regular verbs, and treat them all the same. At the back of this *Manual* you will find a table with the regular endings. There are only four irregular verbs (three highly irregular and one somewhat confusing) that you should know how to conjugate. These are listed after the regular verbs in the Appendix.

2. Verbs are divided into three groups, according to their infinitive (i.e., unconjugated form as in "to take") ending. These endings are **-ar, -er,** and **-ir.** For some reason, there are more verbs ending with -ar than -er or -ir, so when inventing... Also, verbs with -er and -ir endings often have identical conjugations, so when in doubt...

3. We'll get to this after we try our hand at some verbs.

---

[1] There is no subject pronoun "it" in Spanish. Just say the verb without a pronoun. For example, to say:

(it) is wet, simply say: is wet: Está mojado.
(it) is dry, simply say: is dry: Está _____
(it) is hot, simply say: is hot: ____ ____
(it) is cold, simply say: is cold: ____ ____

4.2.3 Doing It

VOCABULARY AND STRESS GUIDE

nouns

la botella	the bottle
la tableta	the tablet, pill
las vitaminas	the vitamins
el hierro	the iron

verbs

Pepe toma	Pepe takes
Pepe abre	Pepe opens
Pepe pone	Pepe puts
Pepe mastica	Pepe chews
Pepe bebe	Pepe drinks
Pepe traga	Pepe swallows
Pepe cierra	Pepe closes

¿Qué es?   Es la botella de Pepe.
La botella de Pepe es pequeña.
La botella de Pepe está encima de la mesa.
¿Cómo es la botella de Pepe?   _____.
¿Dónde está la botella de Pepe?   _____.

¿Qué es?   Es la tableta.
La tableta es pequeña.
La tableta es blanca.
¿Cómo es la tableta?   _____.
¿De qué color es la tableta?   _____.

¿Qué es?   Es un vaso de agua.
El vaso de agua está encima de la mesa.
¿Dónde está el vaso de agua?   _____.

Pepe **toma** la botella.
Pepe _____ la botella.

¿Toma Pepe la venda?   No, Pepe no _____.
¿Toma Pepe el vaso de agua?   No, _____.
¿Qué toma Pepe?   _____.

Pepe **abre** la botella.
Pepe _____ la botella.

¿Abre Pepe la boca?   No, Pepe no _____.
¿Abre Pepe la mano?   No, _____.
¿Qué abre Pepe?   _____.

Pepe _____ la botella y toma la tableta de la botella.

¿Toma Pepe un lápiz de la botella? No, Pepe no _____.
¿Toma Pepe una venda de la botella? No, _____.
¿Qué toma Pepe de la botella?   _____.

Pepe **pone** la tableta en la boca.
Pepe _____ la tableta en la boca.

¿Pone Pepe la tableta en la botella? No, Pepe no _____.
¿Pone Pepe la tableta debajo de
  la mesa?   No, _____.
¿Dónde pone Pepe la tableta?   _____.

Pepe **mastica** la tableta.
Pepe _____ la tableta.

¿Mastica Pepe la botella?   No, Pepe no _____.
¿Mastica Pepe la mesa?   No, _____.
¿Qué mastica Pepe?   _____.

Pepe _____ el vaso de agua.
Pepe **bebe** el agua.
Pepe _____ el agua.

¿Bebe Pepe Coca-Cola?   No, Pepe no _____.
¿Bebe Pepe vino?   No, _____.
¿Qué bebe Pepe?   _____.

Pepe **traga** la tableta y el agua.
Pepe _____ la tableta y el agua.

¿Traga Pepe las vitaminas?   No, Pepe no _____.
¿Traga Pepe la tableta de hierro? No, _____.
¿Qué traga Pepe?   _____.

(say: Pepe puts the glass of water on top of the table)

_____. (wow!)

Pepe **cierra** la botella.
Pepe _____ la botella.

¿Cierra Pepe la boca?   No, Pepe no _____.
¿Cierra Pepe el ojo?   No, _____.
¿Qué cierra Pepe?

_____.

(say: Pepe puts the bottle on top of the table)

_____.

4.2.4 Conjugation Tables

Now you're ready for:

    3. How to conjugate a verb.

INFINITIVE =	ROOT +	ENDING
tomar =	**tom-** + (to take)	**- a r**
beber =	**beb-** + (to drink)	**- e r**
abrir =	**abr-** + (to open)	**- i r**

First, take the infinitive and lift off the ending, leaving the root behind.
To this root, add the ending that corresponds to the group (-ar, -er, or -ir),
to the person (yo, usted, él, ella) and tense (present, past, etc.).

This is easily done if you have a Cuisinart, but, if you don't, use the
following table:

ENDINGS FOR THE PRESENT TENSE

Pronoun	-ar	-er	-ir
yo	-o	-o	-o
él ella usted	-a	-e	-e

For example, if you want to say "I take," you have to:

1. take the infinitive **tomar**
2. lift off ending **tom-** **ar**
3. keep the root **tom-**
4. add ending for
-ar group
  yo
  present } **-o**
5. and you get **yo tomo** (I take)

If you want to say "he takes," you have to:

1. take the infinitive **tomar**
2. lift off ending **tom-** **ar**
3. keep the root **tom-**
4. add ending for
-ar group
  él
  present } **-a**
5. and you get **él toma** (he takes)

If you want to say "she takes," you have to:

1. take the infinitive **tomar**
2. lift off ending   **tom-**   **ar**
3. keep the root   **tom-**
4. add ending for

-ar group ⎫
   ella   ⎬   **-a**
 present ⎭

5. and you get   **ella toma** (she takes)

If you want to say "you take," you have to:

1. take the infinitive **tomar**
2. lift off ending   **tom-**   **ar**
3. keep the root   **tom-**
4. add ending for

-ar group ⎫
  usted ⎬   **-a**
 present ⎭

5. and you get   **usted toma** (you take)

If you want to say "I drink," you have to

1. take the infinitive **beber**
2. lift off ending   **beb-**   **er**
3. keep the root   **beb-**
4. add ending for

-er group ⎫
   yo   ⎬   **-o**
 present ⎭

5. and you get   **yo bebo** (I drink)

If you want to say "he drinks," you have to:

1. take the infinitive **beber**
2. lift off ending **beb-** **er**
3. keep the root **beb-**
4. add ending for
-er group ⎤
    él ⎬ **-e**
 present ⎦
5. and you get **él bebe** (he drinks)

If you want to say "she drinks," you have to:

1. take the infinitive **beber**
2. lift off ending **beb-** **er**
3. keep the root **beb-**
4. add ending for
-er group ⎤
  ella ⎬ **-e**
 present ⎦
5. and you get **ella bebe** (she drinks)

If you want to say "you drink," you have to:

1. take the infinitive **beber**
2. lift off ending **beb-** **er**
3. keep the root **beb-**
4. add ending for
-er group ⎤
  usted ⎬ **-e**
 present ⎦
5. and you get **usted bebe** (you drink)

If you want to say "I open," you have to:

1. take the infinitive **abrir**
2. lift off ending   **abr-**   **ir**
3. keep the root   **abr-**
4. add ending for
 -ir group ⎱
    yo   ⎬   **-o**
  present ⎰
5. and you get   **yo abro** (I open)

If you want to say "he opens," you have to:

1. take the infinitive **abrir**
2. lift off ending   **abr-**   **ir**
3. keep the root   **abr-**
4. add ending for
 -ir group ⎱
    él   ⎬   **-e**
  present ⎰
5. and you get   **él abre** (he opens)

If you want to say "she opens," you have to:

1. take the infinitive **abrir**
2. lift off ending   **abr-**   **ir**
3. keep the root   **abr-**
4. add ending for
 -ir group ⎱
    ella   ⎬   **-e**
  present ⎰
5. and you get   **ella abre** (she opens)

If you want to say "you open," you have to:

1. take the inifinitive **abrir**
2. lift off ending   **abr-   ir**
3. keep the root   **abr-**
4. add ending for
 -ir group ⎤
   usted ⎬   **-e**
   present ⎦
5. and you get   **usted abre** (you open)

4.2.5 Doing It Some More

VOCABULARY AND STRESS GUIDE

nouns
el español   the Spanish
el inglés   the English
el antibiótico   the antibiotic
el elevador/ascensor   the elevator
la leche   the milk
el azúcar   the sugar

verbs
hablar   to speak
toser   to cough
vivir   to live
fumar   to smoke

conjunctions
con   with
sin   without

I promise not to give you many of these exercises, but sometimes, like medicine, they're good for you.

INFINITIVO	YO	ÉL, ELLA, USTED
tomar	yo tomo	él toma
masticar	yo _____	él _____
tragar	_____	_____
cerrar	yo cierr_*	él cierr_*
hablar	_____	_____
beber	yo bebo	él bebe
toser	_____	_____
poner	yo pong_*	_____
abrir	yo abro	él abre
vivir	_____	_____

*irregular root

Translate into Spanish:
I speak Spanish.   _____ español.
You speak Spanish   _____.
Speak you English?   _____ inglés?
Speak you English or Spanish?   _____.
Take you vitamins?   _____.
Take you iron?   _____.
What antibiotics take you?   ____ antibióticos _____.
I take the elevator.   _____.
I smoke.   Yo fumo.
Do you smoke?   _____.
Put you the tablet under your
  tongue?   _____.
Live you in Los Angeles?   _____.
Live you with your mother?   ____ con _____.
Live you with your spouse?   _____.
Live you without your family?   ____ sin _____.

Live you without your son?   _____.
Your son lives with your daughter
   in El Salvador?   _____.
Take you coffee?   _____.
Take you coffee with or without
   milk?   _____ leche?
Take you coffee with sugar?   _____ azúcar?
Take you tea without sugar?   _____.

4.3 KEY CONCEPTS

¿toma usted medicamentos?
¿habla usted inglés?

Lesson 4

La charla
(The Chat)

Translate into Spanish:

Good afternoon, how are you? Would you like some coffee? Would you like coffee with or without milk? With or without sugar?

_____ .

_____ .

I live in El Paso. And you, where do you live? Where are you from? Are you from Central America or from South America? Are you from a big country or a small country? Is your country next to Guatemala? I speak a little bit of Spanish, and do you speak English? You don't speak English, but the boy speaks English, correct?

_____ .

_____ .

_____ .

_____ .

Does the boy cough? I'm sorry. Do you smoke? Do you smoke in front of the boy? Does your husband smoke? Does he smoke next to the boy? No, thank you, I don't smoke.

_____ .

_____ .

Do you live in a house? Is the house big or small? Do you live with your family? Does your daughter live in the house with you? Does your son live with you or in your country?

_____ .

_____ .

Nice meeting you! Good-by and good luck!

_____ .

La charla

Buenas tardes, ¿cómo está? ¿Quiere café? ¿Quiere café con o sin leche? ¿Con o sin azúcar?

Yo vivo en El Paso. Y usted, ¿dónde vive? ¿De dónde es usted? ¿Es usted de Centro América o de Sud América? ¿Es usted de un país grande o pequeño? ¿Está su país al lado de Guatemala? Yo hablo un poco de español, y usted ¿habla inglés? Usted no habla inglés, pero el niño habla inglés, ¿verdad?

¿Tose el niño? Lo siento. ¿Fuma usted? ¿Fuma usted delante del niño? ¿Fuma su esposo? ¿Fuma él al lado del niño? No gracias, no fumo.

¿Vive usted en una casa? ¿Es grande o pequeña la casa? ¿Vive usted con su familia? ¿Vive su hija en la casa con usted? ¿Vive su hijo con usted o en su país?

¡Mucho gusto! ¡Adiós y buena suerte!

Now, go back to page 4 and look at the "Herpes" paragraph again. How much more can you understand?

Lesson 5. The Verb "To Have"

5.1 THE IRREGULAR VERB "TO GO"

VOCABULARY AND STRESS GUIDE

nouns

la clínica	the clinic
la obs<u>te</u>tra	the obstetrician
la ofi<u>ci</u>n a	the office
la mandíbula	the jaw

verbs

Ana va a	Ana goes to

interrogatives

¿Adónde ...?	Where to?

We're about to learn one of those highly irregular verbs, but fortunately, it is short and simple to pronounce. While we're on the subject, "v" is pronounced like "**b**," as in **B**irginia and **B**alium.

As in English, the verb **ir** (to go) always takes the preposition "to," which in Spanish is **a.** (For those of you who think the preposition "to" is the "to" of "to go," it's not. It's the "to" of "to go <u>to</u>....")

Ana **va a** la clínica de la obstetra.
Ana __ _ la clínica de la _____
Pepe __ _ la clínica _____

¿Va Ana a la oficina?   No, Ana no _____.
¿Va Ana a su casa?   No, _____.
¿Adónde va Ana?   _____.

Ana va a la cínica con Pepe.
¿Va Ana a la clínica con Juan?   No, Ana no _____.
¿Con quién va Ana a la clínica?   _____.
¿Adónde va Pepe?   _____.

Juan no va a la clínica, Juan va **al**[1] hospital.
Juan va al hospital con el Señor Gomez.
¿Adónde va Juan?   _____.
¿Adónde va el Señor Gomez?   _____.

El dolor va al brazo izquierdo.
¿Va el dolor al brazo derecho?   _____.
¿Va el dolor a la pierna derecha?   _____.
¿Va el dolor a la nariz?   _____.
_____ va el dolor?   El dolor va al brazo izquierdo.
_____?   El dolor va a la espalda.
_____?   El dolor va a la mandíbula.

¿Adónde va usted?   **Yo voy** a la clínica.
¿Adónde va usted?   _____ a mi casa.
¿Adónde va usted?   _____ al hospital.

5.2 PUTTING IT ALL TOGETHER

VOCABULARY AND STRESS GUIDE

nouns
el ca<u>lor</u>   the warmth
la sensación   the sensation

Translate into Spanish:
Where is the pain?   ¿Dónde _____?
To where goes the pain?   ¿Adónde _____?
Where is the warmth?   _____?

---

[1]a + el = al (but a + él = a él).
 a + la = a la.

To where goes the warmth?	_____.
Where is the sensation?	_____.
To where goes the sensation?	_____.
Where is the sensation in your chest?	_____.
To where goes the sensation in your chest?	_____.

5.3 WHY? BECAUSE!

VOCABULARY AND STRESS GUIDE

nouns

el calmante	the sedative
el baño	the bathroom

adjectives

sentado/a	sitting
cansado/a	tired
de pie	standing
dormido/a	asleep
triste	sad
contento/a	happy
preocupado/a	worried
deprimido/a	depressed
débil	weak
último/a	last

interrogatives

¿por qué?	why?

conjunction

porque	because

Just repeat and don't think:

Pepe toma aspirina **porque** está enfermo.
Pepe toma aspirina _____ está enfermo.
Pepe toma aspirina _____ ___ enfermo.

¿Toma Pepe aspirina porque
  está bien?   No, Pepe no _____.

¿Toma Pepe aspirina porque
  está sano?   No, _____.

¿Por qué toma Pepe aspirina?   Pepe toma aspirina **porque** está ____.

¿Por qué toma Pepe medicamentos?   Pepe toma medicamentos _____.

____ ____ toma Pepe calmantes?   Pepe toma calmantes porque está
                                   nervioso.

____ ____ toma Pepe antibióticos?   Pepe toma antibióticos ____ está mal.

____ ____ está Pepe sentado?   Pepe está sentado ____ está cansado.

____ ____ está Ana de pie?   Ana está de pie ____ no está cansada.

____ ____ va Juan a la cama?   Juan va a la cama ____ está cansado.

____ ____ está Juan en la cama?   Juan está en la cama ____ está dormido.

____ ____ no está Ana en la cama?   Ana no está en la cama ____ no está
                                   dormida.

____ ____ está Pepe triste?   Pepe está triste ____ está enfermo.

____ ____ está Ana contenta?   Ana está contenta ____ no está enferma.

____ ____ está Pepe preocupado?   Pepe está preocupado ____ está enfermo.

____ ____ está Juan cansado?   Juan está cansado ____ está deprimido.

____ ____ está Ana contenta?   Ana está contenta ____ está fuerte.[2]

____ ____ está Pepe deprimido?   Pepe está deprimido ____ está débil.

Here we are again, confronted by yet another grammatical cruelty. In Spanish,
"why?" and "because" are the same word: **¿Por qué?** and **porque.** Notice
that "why?" is written as two words and carries an accent and "because" is
one word without an accent.

Translate into Spanish:

Why are you depressed?   _____.

Why is your mother tired?   _____.

Why not is your mother more
  strong?   _____.

Why do you take medicaments?   _____.

Why don't you take the last
  medicament?   _____.

Why don't you go to the bathroom?   _____.

---

[2]Ana is strong (as in, after an operation, i.e., temporarily) you say "Ana está fuerte."
Ana is strong (as in, she works out everyday lifting weights, i.e., permanently) you say
"Ana es fuerte." This all became clear to you in Lesson 3, remember?

Why don't you go to the last
bathroom with the nurse?   _____.

5.4 THE VERB "TENER"

VOCABULARY AND STRESS GUIDE

nouns

la diarrea	the diarrhea
la náusea	the nausea
los vómitos	the vomiting
la anemia	the anemia
la tos	the cough
la fiebre	the fever
la gastritis	the gastritis
la bronquitis	the bronchitis
la apendicitis	the appendicitis
la hepatitis	the hepatitis
la diabetes	the diabetes
la hipertensión	the hypertension
la tuberculosis	the tuberculosis
la pancreatitis	the pancreatitis
la artritis	the arthritis
la celulitis	the cellulitis

adjectives

rosado/a	pink
oscuro/a	dark

verb

yo tengo	I have
usted tiene	you have

adverb

mal	poorly
verdaderamente	really

Juan	Pepe

Juan

¿Cómo está, Pepe?
¿Porqué está mal, Pepe?
¿Tiene usted dolor de cabeza?
¿Tiene usted dolor de espalda?
___ ____ dolor de estómago?
___ ____ diarrea?
___ ____ náusea?
___ ____ vómitos?
___ ____ anemia?
___ ____ tos?
___ ____ fiebre?
_____?
(Have you nausea with the pain?)
_____?
(Have you pink vomiting?)
_____?
(Have you fever with the pain?)
_____?
(Have you pain with the cough?)
_____?
(Have you dark urine?)
¡Pobre Pepe! ¡Usted está
   verdaderamente enfermo!

Pepe

Mal, Juan, muy mal.

¡Sí!
¡Sí!
¡Sí!
¡Sí!
¡Sí!
¡Sí!
¡Sí!
¡Sí!
¡Sí!

¡Sí, **yo tengo** náusea con el dolor!

Sí, _____.

Sí, _____.

Sí, _____.

Sí, _____.

¡Sí, pobre de mí!

This is another one of those misbehaved verbs. **Tener** (to have) is conjugated as follows:

TENER
yo tengo   I have
usted tiene   you have
él tiene   he has
ella tiene   she has
--tiene   it has

Almost any complaint, illness, or condition can be linked up with this verb. Keeping in mind that 1) words ending in **-ion, -itis** and **-osis** in English are the same in Spanish; 2) "th" in Spanish doesn't exist (just drop the "h");

3) never pronounce "h"; 4) "ph" is pronounced exactly as it is in English, but written with an "f"; and 5) "do" and "does" do not exist!!, translate the following into Spanish:

Do you have anemia?   _____.
Do you have gastritis?   _____.
Do you have bronchitis?   _____.
Do you have appendicitis?   _____.
Do you have hepatitis?   _____.
Do you have diabetes?   _____.
Do you have hypertension?   _____.
Does your father have tuberculosis?   _____.
Do you have pancreatitis?   _____.
Does your mother have pancreatitis?   _____.
Do you have arthritis?   _____.
Does your grandmother have
   arthritis?   _____.
Do you have cellulitis? So what!   _____.

5.5 FOR HOW LONG ....?

VOCABULARY AND STRESS GUIDE

nouns
el segundo	the second
el minuto	the minute
la hora	the hour
el día	the day
la semana	the week
el mes	the month
al año	the year
el calambre	the cramp
la escuela	the school

adjectives
uno	one
dos	two
tres	three

In case any of you out there in Espanishlandia are thinking, please don't. This next section works best if your mind is out to lunch. It helps, though, if you know the following vocabulary:

el segundo	**the second**
el minuto	**the minute**
la hora	**the hour**
el día	**the day**
la semana	**the week**
el mes	**the month**
el año	**the year**
el ano	**the anus**
uno	**one**
dos	**two**
tres	**three**

Juan

¿Vive usted en México?

¿Vive usted en los Estados Unidos muchos años?

¿**Hace cuánto** vive usted en los Estados Unidos?

¿Vive usted con Pepita?

¿**Hace cuánto** vive usted con Pepita?

¿Habla usted inglés?

¿**Hace cuánto** habla usted inglés?

¿Toma medicamentos usted?

¿**Hace cuánto** toma usted medicamentos?

¿Tiene dolor de estómago?

¿**Hace cuánto** tiene dolor de estómago?

¿Tiene vómitos?

_____ _____ tiene vómitos?

¿Tiene fiebre?

_____ _____ tiene fiebre?

_____ náusea?

_____ _____ tiene náusea?

Pepe

¡No, hombre! ¡Yo vivo en los Estados Unidos!

¡Sí, **hace** 3 años!

Hace ___ años.

Sí, yo vivo con Pepita.

_____ 3 años.

Sí, yo hablo inglés.

_____ 3 años.

Sí, yo tomo medicamentos.

_____ 2 años.

Sí, tengo dolor de estómago.

_____ 2 semanas.

Sí, tengo vómitos.

Hace 3 días.

Sí, tengo fiebre.

Hace 3 días.

Sí, tengo náusea.

Hace 2 días.

_____ calambres?   Sí, tengo calambres.
_____ _____ ___ calambres?   Hace 1 día.
_____ orina oscura?   Sí, tengo _____
_____ _____ ___ orina oscura?   Hace 2 semanas.

So, how was lunch? I know, you shouldn't have had that Burrito with the extra sauce and Frijoles because now you feel like going to the sala de emergencia to get your estómago pumped. So you get to the E.R. and someone who's been on duty 36 hours asks you:

Have you pain?
For how long have you pain?
Have you vomiting?
For how long have you vomiting?
Have you fever?
For how long have you fever?

Or, if the person has been on duty for 36 hours and studying medical Spanish for another 10 (it was a slow night), they'd ask:

¿Tiene dolor?
¿Hace cuánto tiene dolor?
¿Tiene vómitos?
¿Hace cuánto tiene vómitos?
¿Tiene fiebre?
¿Hace cuánto tiene fiebre?

The answer to the second question, "Hace cuánto tiene...?" will always be:

HACE __ segundo(s)
HACE __ minuto(s)
HACE __ hora(s)
HACE __ día(s)
HACE __ semana(s)
HACE __ mes(es)
HACE __ año(s)

Memorize this by heart:

¿Tiene X?
¿Tiene dolor?
¿Tiene fiebre?
¿Tiene vómitos?
¿_____ náusea?
Do you have cramps?
_____?
Do you have pain in the chest?

_____?

¿Hace cuánto tiene X?
¿Hace cuánto tiene dolor?
¿Hace cuánto tiene _____?
_____?
_____?
For how long do you have cramps?
_____?
For how long do you have pain in the
    chest?

_____?

¿Toma X?
¿Toma medicamentos?
_____ antibióticos?
_____ drogas (drugs,
    usually illicit)

¿Hace cuánto toma X?
¿Hace cuánto toma medicamentos?
_____?

_____?

¿Any verb X?
Do you smoke?
_____?
Do you live in Santa Fe?
_____?
Do you go to school?
_____?

¿Hace cuánto any verb X?
For how long do you smoke?
_____?
For how long do you live in Santa Fe?
_____?
For how long do you go to school?
_____?

The above is an important section. If you were asleep or watching "I Love Lucy" re-runs, please wake up and/or turn off the T.V. Repeat this section.

5.6 HOW MANY TIMES?

VOCABULARY AND STRESS GUIDE

nouns

el bebé	the baby
la vez/las veces	the time/the times
la leche de pecho	the breast milk
la mamadera	the bottle (baby's)
la contracción	the contraction
las bebidas alcohólicas	the alcoholic drinks (alcohol)

adjectives

cu<u>a</u>tro	four
<u>cinc</u>o	five
regu<u>lar</u>	regular
<u>ca</u>da	each/every
<u>mu</u>cho/a	many

verbs

elim<u>inar</u>	to	eliminate/defecate
ori<u>nar</u>	to	urinate
dar el <u>pe</u>cho	to	breast feed
mo<u>ver</u> el vi<u>e</u>ntre	to	move the bowels

El bebé toma leche 5 **veces** por día.
El bebé toma leche 5 _____ __ día.

¿Toma leche el bebé 4 veces por día?	No, el bebé no _____
¿Toma leche el bebé 3 veces por día?	No, el bebé no _____
¿Cuántas veces toma leche el bebé por día?	El bebé toma leche _____
¿Cuántas veces toma agua el bebé por día?	_____ 2 _____
¿Cuántas veces toma leche de pecho por día?	_____ 3 _____
_____ ___ toma formula por día?	_____ 3 _____
_____ ___ toma la mamadera por día?	_____ 3 _____
_____ ___ elimina por día?	_____ 4 _____
_____ ___ orina por día?	_____ 5 _____
_____ ___ toma vitaminas por día?	Toma vitaminas **1 vez**[3] por día.
_____ ___ da el pecho la mamá?	_____ 3 _____

---

[3]Una **vez** means one time; tres **veces** means three times.

Translate into Spanish:

How many times do you urinate
    per night?   _____?

How many times do you eliminate
    per day?   _____?

How many times do you move
    your bowels?   _____?

How many times do you move
    your arm?   _____?

How many times do you
    breast feed?   _____?

How many times do you take
    tablets?   _____?

How many times do you have
    contractions?   _____?

How many times do you have
    regular contractions?   _____?

Every 5 minutes?   _____?

How many times does the baby
    drink breast milk?   _____?

Every two hours?   _____?

How many times do you drink
    alcohol?   _____?

Many times?   _____?

One time?   _____?

5.7 KEY CONCEPTS

¿Por qué?
¿Tiene dolor?
¿Hace cuánto tiene dolor?
¿Adónde va el dolor?
¿Cuántas veces?
Una vez

Lesson 5

La mujer embarazada
(The Pregnant Woman)

(translate this out loud)   **(check yourself with this)**

Good day. How are you?   Buenos días. ¿Cómo está?
I call myself ____   Me llamo ____
I am the obstetrician, nurse,   Yo soy el/la obstetra, el/la enfermero/a,
  medical student.   el/la estudiante de medicina.
How do you call yourself?   ¿Cómo se llama usted?
Glad to meet you.   Mucho gusto.

Are you pregnant?   ¿Está usted embarazada?
Do you have periods regular?   ¿Tiene períodos regulares?
Your last period?   ¿Su último período?

Do you have relations sexual?   ¿Tiene relaciones sexuales?
Do you use contraception? Which?   ¿Usa contracepción? ¿Cuál?
How many children do you have?   ¿Cuántos hijos tiene?
You have[4] problems with your last   ¿Usted tiene problemas con su último
  pregnancy? You have abortions?   embarazo? ¿Tiene abortos?
You have a Cesarian? Why?   ¿Tiene una Cesárea? ¿Por qué?

Is your chest (breast) different?   ¿Está su pecho diferente?
Is it more large? With more pain?   ¿Está más grande? ¿Con más dolor?
With nodules? Is the   ¿Con nódulos? ¿Está la
  areola more dark?   areola más oscura?
Is the areola more large?   ¿Está la areola más grande?

Are you tired? Are you more tired?   ¿Está cansada? ¿Está más cansada?
Are you weak? Are you more weak?   ¿Está débil? ¿Está más débil?
Do you have nausea?   ¿Tiene náusea?
Do you have vomiting?   ¿Tiene vómitos?
For how long do you have nausea?   ¿Hace cuánto tiene náusea?

---

[4]I am utilizing the present tense instead of the preterit (past) because we have not yet learned it; you will be understood.

Do you urinate at night?	¿Orina usted a la noche?
How many times do you urinate per night?	¿Cuántas veces orina usted por noche?
Do you have pain with the urine?[5]	¿Tiene dolor con la orina?
Does the baby move?	¿Mueve[6] el bebé?
Does the baby move at night?	¿El bebé mueve a la noche?
Do you have blood from the vagina?	¿Tiene sangre de la vagina?
Much?	¿Mucha?
Do you have cramps in the uterus?	¿Tiene calambres en el útero?
Do you have cramps in the legs?	¿Tiene calambres en las piernas?
Do you have contractions?	¿Tiene contracciones?
Are[7] the contractions regular?	¿Son las contracciones regulares?
For how long do you have contractions?	¿Hace cuánto tiene contracciones?
Do you have pain?	¿Tiene dolor?
Where is the pain?	¿Dónde está el dolor?
Do you have pain in the legs?	¿Tiene dolor en las piernas?
Do you have water from the vagina?	¿Tiene agua de la vagina?
For how long do you have water from the vagina? What color is the water? Is the water pink?	¿Hace cuánto tiene agua de la vagina? ¿De qué color es el agua? ¿Es el agua rosada?
Is the water red? Brown or green?	¿Es roja? ¿Marrón o verde?
Do you take medication? Why?	¿Toma medicamentos? ¿Por qué?
Do you take vitamins? Iron?	¿Toma vitaminas? ¿Toma hierro?
Do you have hypertension?	¿Tiene hipertensión?
Diabetes? Hepatitis? Herpes?	¿Diabetes? ¿Hepatitis? ¿Herpes?
Problems with the heart or the kidneys? Other problems medical?	¿Problemas con el corazón o los riñones? ¿Otros problemas médicos?
Do you smoke? For how long do you smoke? Do you drink alcoholic beverages? Do you take drugs?	¿Fuma usted? ¿Hace cuánto fuma? ¿Toma usted bebidas alcohólicas? ¿Toma usted drogas?

---

[5]We will learn the correct way later, but for now, if you say this, you will be understood.

[6]Correctly said, "se mueve el bebé?" which is reflexive; more on reflexive verbs in Lesson 12.

[7]We will learn third person plural later; you can either use the third person singular "Es la contracción regular?" or memorize the correct way of saying it now.

Do you want to breastfeed
  or the bottle?

¿Quiere usted dar el pecho
  o la mamadera?

The urine analysis indicates that you are pregnant. Every four weeks you
come to visit the doctor. You come to the clinic with blood from the vagina,
with face or fingers swollen, with severe headache, with problems in the
eyes, with vomiting persistent, with fever, with pain with the urine or with
water from the vagina.

El análisis de orina indica que usted está embarazada. Cada cuatro semanas
usted viene a visitar la doctora. Usted viene a la clínica con sangre de la
vagina, con cara o dedos hinchados, con dolor de cabeza severo, con problemas
en los ojos, con vómitos persistentes, con fiebre, con dolor con la orina, o con
agua de la vagina.

Now, go back to page 4 and look at the "Herpes" paragraph again. How much more can you
understand?

Lesson 6. Time and Counting

6.1 THE NUMBERS

Just about everyone knows how to count to ten in Spanish, right? (For those of you who took French in high school, you will have to work extra hard in this section to learn one through ten.) All you really need to learn then, is 11-15, 20, 30, 40, etc. The other numbers are combinations of the numbers you already know (or will soon know).

1 uno
2 dos
3 tres
4 cuatro
5 cinco
6 seis
7 siete
8 ocho
9 nueve
10 diez

¿Tiene Pepe una nariz? _____.
¿Tiene Pepe dos brazos? _____.
¿Tiene Juan tres piernas? _____.
¿Tiene Juan cuatro manos? _____.
¿Tiene Pepe cinco dedos en
  la mano derecha? _____.
¿Tiene Juan seis dedos en
  la mano izquierda? _____.
¿Tiene Pepe siete cabezas? _____.
¿Tiene Juan ocho tobillos? _____.
¿Tiene Pepe nueve codos? _____.

¿Tiene Juan diez dedos?   _____.

11 on**ce**
12 do**ce**
13 tre ___
14 cator ___
15 quin ___

Diez más uno es igual a   _____.
Diez más dos es igual a   _____.
Diez más tres es igual a   _____.
Diez más cuatro es igual a   _____.
Diez más cinco es igual a   _____.

16 diez y seis
17 diez y siete
18 diez y ___
19 ___ _ ___

Diez más seis es igual a   _____.
Diez más siete es igual a   _____.
Diez más ocho es igual a   _____.
Diez más nueve es igual a   _____.

20 veinte
21 veinte y uno
22 veinte y ___
23 veinte _ ___
25 _____
28 _____
30 treinta
39 _____
40 cuarenta
44 _____
50 cincuenta
57 _____
60 sesenta
66 _____
70 setenta
75 _____
80 ochenta
82 _____
90 noventa

99 _____
100 cien
101 ciento y uno
107 _____ _ ____
200 dos cientos
300 ____ cientos
400 _____
500 quinientos
600 seis _____
700 _____
800 _____
900 _____
1000 mil
2000 dos mil
3467 tres mil cuatro cientos sesenta y ____
5982 _____ _____ _____ _ _____

Anyway, you get the idea, right? Before figuring out how to say the deficit in Spanish, know 1 through 15 well. The rest is practically a repetition of the first ten numbers. When in doubt, use your fingers (one through ten, anyway), write, or mumble. Then call an interpreter.

6.2 WHAT TIME IS IT?

It's not that our watches break, stop, get lost, or run half an hour late, it's that the Latin concept of time allows for longer coffee breaks, unexpected friends, and broken fan belts.   So, how do we tell time in Spanish, other than late? We tell the hour, and not the time. To ask "What time is it?" we say:

What hour **is it?**
 _____ hora_____

If you're having trouble remembering "Is it," remember that it's just one word. Think back on the question "**What is it?**" (_____ __) and substitute in above.

When we answer, we don't say "It is 2 o'clock" (because technically, 2 is plural and it should be "They are 2 o'clocks"). We forget about the o'clocks and the o'learys and simply say:

They are the 2.
Son las[1] 2.

It is 3 o'clock, you'd say   they are the 3
It is 4 o'clock, you'd say   they _____
It is 7 o'clock, you'd say   _____ all the way to midnight

They are the 2   **son las dos** (It is two o'clock)
They are the 3   son __ ___ (It is three o'clock)
They are the 4   __ __ ___ (It is four o'clock)
They are the 5   _____ (It is five o'clock)
They are the 6   _____ (It is six o'clock)
They are the 7   _____ (It is seven o'clock)
They are the 8   _____ (It is eight o'clock)
They are the 9   _____ (It is nine o'clock)
They are the 10   _____ (It is ten o'clock)
They are the 11   _____ (It is eleven o'clock)
They are the 12   _____ (It is twelve o'clock)
It is the 1   **Es la una**

To say the minutes after the hour, say **the number of the hour and the number of the minutes** (without saying the words "horas" or "minutos").

2:05   Son las dos **y** cinco
3:10   Son las ___ _ ____
4:15   __ __ ___ _ _____ (Also: Son las cuatro
               y cuarto)
5:30   __ __ ___ _ _____ (Also: Son las cinco
               y media)
10:35   _____.

To tell the minutes before the hour, say **the number of the hour minus the number of the minutes,** so that "twenty-five to six" becomes six minus twenty-five.

25 to 6   Son las seis **menos** veinte y cinco
20 to 7   __ __ ___ ____ _____
15 to 8   __ __ ___ ____ _____
10 to 9   __ __ ___ ____ _____
5 to 11   __ __ ___ ____ _____

---

[1] **Las** refers to **las horas** which we omit.

Noon, or midday, is translated exactly like "midday" into Spanish:
midday
mediodía

and midnight is also literal:
midnight
medianoche

Why mediodía if día ends with an **a**? And medianoche if noche ends with an **e**? Because I say so. Actually, it's because día is a masculine noun (ergo, **el mediodía**) and noche is a feminine noun (giving us **la medianoche**).

6.3 AT WHAT TIME...?

VOCABULARY AND STRESS GUIDE

nouns

la far<u>ma</u>cia	the pharmacy
el ginecólogo	the gynecologist, m
la ginecóloga	the gynecologist, f
la <u>ci</u>ta	the appointment
el ar<u>dor</u>	the burning
la cin<u>tu</u>ra	the lower back
las <u>nal</u>gas	the buttocks
los <u>mus</u>los	the thighs

verbs

comen<u>zar</u>	to begin
termi<u>nar</u>	to end

Es la hora to start putting some of those old blocks together:

What time (hour)?
____ _____?
The clinic opens.

__ ____ ____

The clinic closes.

__ ____ ____

At what hour opens the clinic?
A __ ___ ____ __ ____?

Translate into Spanish:

At what hour closes the clinic?	_____?
At what hour opens the pharmacy?	_____?
At what hour goes the patient to the hospital?	_____?
At what hour goes your mother to the appointment?	_____ la cita?
At what hour goes your mother to the appointment with the gynecologist?	_____ la ginecóloga?
At what hour commences (begins) the pain?	_____ comienza _____?
At what hour commences the burning?	_____ el ardor?
At what hour terminates (ends) the burning?	_____ termina _____?
At what hour terminates the pain in the lower back?	_____ la cintura[2]?
At what hour commences the pain in the buttocks?	_____ las nalgas?
At what hour terminates the sensation in the thighs?	_____ los muslos?

6.4 AT...

VOCABULARY AND STRESS GUIDE

nouns

el perineo	the perineum

expressions

de la mañana	in the morning
de la tarde	in the afternoon
de la noche	in the evening

To say "It is 2 o'clock," we say

_____

[2]La cintura means waist and lower back.

"They are the 2," or ___ __ ___

To say "At 2 o'clock," we say
"At the 2," or **a** __ ___

At (the) 3:00   A las tres
At (the) 4:00   _____ .
At (the) 5:05   _____ (At the five and five)
At (the) 6:45   _____ (At the seven minus quarter)

Translate into Spanish:
The appointment begins at 8:05   _____ .
The pain in the thighs begins at
   8:05 in the morning.   _____ de la mañana[3]
The appointment with the gynecologist
   ends at 5:00 in the afternoon.   _____ de la tarde.
The burning in the perineum begins
   at the 3:00 in the afternoon.   ____ el perineo _____ .
The burning in the perinuem begins
   at 11:00 in the evening.   _____ de la noche.

6.5 WHEN?

VOCABULARY AND STRESS GUIDE

nouns
el examen   the exam, usu. physical
el tratamiento   the treatment

preposition
en   in

interrogative
¿cuándo?   when?

---

[3]N.B. we use the same word for morning and tomorrow: **mañana**, as in, I'll do it mañana.

Juan	Pepe
¿Pepe, tose usted a la mañana?[4]	No Juan, yo no toso a la mañana.
¿Tose usted a la tarde?	No, yo no toso a la tarde.
¿Cuándo tose usted?	Yo toso a la noche.
_____ tiene vómitos?	Yo tengo vómitos _____ (in the morning)
_____ tiene náusea?	Yo tengo náusea _____ (in the afternoon)
_____ tiene dolor en la cintura?	Yo tengo dolor en la cintura _____ (in the evening)
_____ tiene la sensación en los muslos?	Yo tengo la sensación en los muslos _____ (in the morning)
_____ comienza la cita con el doctor?	La cita con el doctor comienza **en** 5 minutos.
_____ termina el examen?	El examen termina _____ (in 15 minutes)
_____ comienza el tratamiento?	El tratamiento comienza _____ (in one month)

6.6 BEFORE, AFTER

VOCABULARY AND STRESS GUIDE

nouns

el método de contracepción	the contraception method
el diafragma	the diaphragam
la jalea	the jelly
la vagina	the vagina
el aparato intrauterino	the IUD
las relaciones sexuales	the sexual relations
la posición	the position
el condón	the condom
el pene	the penis
la espuma	the foam
la píldora	the pill

---

[4]Note that in Spanish we say, "Pepe coughs *at* the morning" (Pepe tose a la mañana), and not "*in* the morning." However, we do say, "The appointment begins *in* five minutes" (La cita comienza en cinco minutos).

adjectives

otro/a   other

adverbs

tampoco   neither
también   also

verbs

usar   to use
chequear   to check

prepositions

antes de   before
después de   after

Pepe va a la clínica de la doctora con Pepita. La doctora es una ginecóloga. Pepe quiere un método de contracepción porque él no usa contracepción. Pepita no usa contracepción **tampoco**. Pepita quiere un método de contracepción **también**.

Pepe: Yo quiero un método de contracepción, doctora. Yo no tengo un método.
Pepita: Yo quiero un método de contracepción también.
Dra: ¿Usted conoce el diafragma?
Pepe: Noooooo....
Dra: Bueno, el diafragma está aquí con la jalea .
Pepe: AAAAAAAA...
Dra: Pepita pone el diafragma en la vagina.
Pepe: ¿Y la jalea?
Dra: Pepita pone la jalea encima del diafragma **antes de** poner el diafragma en la vagina. Ella pone la jalea, y **después de** poner la jalea, ella pone el diafragma en la vagina. Éste es otro método. Se llama el aparato intrauterino. El aparato va en el útero. Ella chequea la posición del aparato **antes de** tener relaciones sexuales con usted. Éste es otro método. El condón. El condón va en el pene. Usted pone el condón en el pene _____ __ tener relaciones sexuales.
Pepita: ¿Y la jalea?
Dra: Usted usa jalea o espuma con el condón. Pero usted tiene relaciones sexuales _____ __ poner la jalea o la espuma en la vagina. Éste es otro método. La píldora. Pepita toma la píldora una vez por día.
Pepe: ¿Cuándo toma Pepita la píldora?
Dra: No es importante cuándo, pero sí es importante tomar la píldora una vez por día.

You've gotten as far as understanding that **antes de** means "before," and that **después de** means "after"? Good. You see, I slipped in two more prepositions without you even noticing. Back in Lesson 4, we learned those other all-too-quickly-forgotten words such as encima de, debajo de, etc de, remember? Those were prepositions, too. Whenever you use a preposition before a verb, that verb always (that's right, no exceptions), always, always remains as an infinitive (we do, however, conjugate the verb preceding the preposition).

6.6.1 Exercises

VOCABULARY AND STRESS GUIDE

nouns

el ven<u>e</u>no	the poison
las <u>par</u>tes pri<u>va</u>das	the private parts (genitals)

verbs

respi<u>rar</u>	to breathe
ori<u>nar</u>	to urinate
eliminar	to eliminate
traba<u>jar</u>	to work
limpi<u>ar</u>	to clean
co<u>mer</u>	to eat
compren<u>der</u>	to understand
apren<u>der</u>	to learn
ve<u>nir</u>	to come
su<u>frir</u>	to suffer

antes de tomar	(before taking, literally, before to take)
_____ __ cerrar	(before closing)
_____ __ _____	(before chewing)
_____ __ _____	(before swallowing)
_____ __ _____	(before commencing)
_____ __ respir __	(before breathing)
_____ __ orin ____	(before urinating)
_____ __ elimin __	(before eliminating)
_____ __ trabaj __	(before working)
_____ __ limpi ___	(before cleaning)

después de tener		(after having)
_____ __ poner		(after putting)
_____ __ _____		(after drinking)
_____ __ _____		(after moving)
_____ __ _____		(after coughing)
_____ __ com___		(after eating)
_____ __ comprend_		(after understanding)
_____ __ aprend_		(after learning)
_____ __ abrir		(before opening)
_____ __ ven___		(after coming)
_____ __ _____		(before going)
_____ __ _____		(after living)
_____ __ suf___		(before suffering)

With a little bit of imagination, you should be able to build the following sentences:

Before commencing the treatment. _____.

Before understanding how to take
the medicament. _____.

After swallowing the venom. _____.

After cleaning your private parts. _____.

After living in El Salvador with
your mother. _____.

6.7 EXPRESSIONS

¡Usted tiene un bebé! **¡Felicitaciones!**

Usted no está bien, pero tampoco no está mal. ¿Está usted **más o menos**?

Usted está enfermo, **por eso** está en la cama.

¡Hola! ¿Qué tal?

6.8 KEY CONCEPTS

¿Qué hora es?
¿A qué hora...?
¿Cuándo?

Lesson 6

La clínica de planeo familiar
(The Family Planning Clinic)

(Read this dialogue, then fill in the missing parts in the dialogue below)

Pepita: Juanita, ¿a qué hora abre la clínica?

Juanita: A las 9 de la mañana.

Pepita: ¿Qué hora es?

Juanita: Son las 9 menos 5. La clínica abre en 5 minutos.

Pepita: Yo quiero un método de contracepción, no uso un método y no quiero estar embarazada.[5]

Juanita: Yo también quiero un método de contracepción; tampoco quiero tener un bebé.

Pepita: ¿Trabaja usted después de la cita con la ginecóloga, o come usted?

Juanita: Yo como después de la cita y antes de trabajar.

Pepita: Aquí está la ginecóloga. Son las nueve y la clínica abre.

Doctora: Buenos dias, Señora Pepita, ¿cómo está?

Pepita: Más o menos, doctora, tengo ardor en las partes privadas.

Doctora: ¿Hace cuánto tiene ardor en el perineo?

Pepita: Hace 3 semanas.

Doctora: ¿El Señor Pepe tiene ardor también?

Pepita: No, él no tiene ardor.

Doctora: ¿Tiene usted dolor cuando orina o elimina?

Pepita: No, no tengo dolor.

Doctora: ¿Usa usted un método de contracepción?

Pepita: No, no uso.

Doctora: ¿Usted conoce el diafragma y la jalea? ¿El condón y la espuma? ¿La píldora o el aparato?

Pepita: Sí, más o menos.

Doctora: Es importante aprender, pero antes de comenzar con usted yo hablo un poco con la Señora Juanita.

---

[5]Correctly said, no quiero **quedar** embarazada.

Fill in

Pepita: Juanita, ¿_____ abre la clínica?

Juanita: A las 9 _____.

Pepita: ¿Qué hora es?

Juanita: Son las 9 menos 5. La clínica abre _____.

Pepita: Yo quiero un método de contracepción, no uso un método y no quiero estar embarazada.

Juanita: Yo _____ quiero un método de contracepción; _____ quiero tener un bebé.

Pepita: ¿Trabaja usted después de la cita con la ginecóloga, o come usted?

Juanita: Yo como _____ la cita y _____ trabajar.

Pepita: Aquí está la ginecóloga. Son las nueve y la clínica abre.

Doctora: Buenos dias, Señora Pepita, ¿cómo está?

Pepita: Más o menos, doctora, tengo ardor en las partes privadas.

Doctora: ¿_____ tiene ardor en el perineo?

Pepita: _____ 3 semanas.

Doctora: ¿El Señor Pepe tiene ardor _____?

Pepita: No, él no tiene ardor.

Doctora: ¿Tiene usted dolor _____ orina o elimina?

Pepita: No, no tengo dolor.

Doctora: ¿Usa usted un _____ de contracepción?

Pepita: No, no uso.

Doctora: ¿Usted conoce el _____ y la jalea? ¿El _____ y la espuma? ¿La píldora o el aparato?

Pepita: Sí, más o menos.

Doctora: Es importante aprender, pero antes de _____ con usted yo hablo un poco con la Señora Juanita.

Now, go back to page 4 and look at the "Herpes" paragraph again. How much more can you understand?

Lesson 7. The Imperative

7.1 COGNATES

If you are the typical Spanish student, you're probably wondering why on earth the Spanish made **enfermo, enfermedad,** and **enfermera** so similar. Am I right, or what?   I hope the following hints will help:

1.   Words that in English end with the **suffix -ity** retain their *roots* but **change -ity to -idad.** (Also note that they are all feminine.) **La enfermedad** is a noun which means the illness.

university becomes	la univers**idad**
abnormal**ity** becomes	la abnormal____
capacity becomes	la _____
debility becomes	__ _____
deformity becomes	__ _____
difficulty becomes	__ _____
possibility becomes	__ _____
regularity becomes	__ _____
infirmity becomes	__ _____ Well, not exactly, but if you say it quickly enough, it sounds as it should: *la enfermedad*, which means the illness.

2.   **Enfermo** is a masculine adjective which means sick, and **enferma** is a feminine adjective which means sick.

Pepe está enferm**o** means	_____.
Rosa está enferm**a** means	_____.
El Señor Lopez está _____ means	Mr. Lopez is sick.
La Señora Lopez está ____ means	Mrs. Lopez is sick.

3.   **El enfermo** is a noun which means the sick man and **la enferma** is a noun which means the sick woman.

El enfermo está en el hospital   _____.
La enferma está en el hospital   _____.
_____ tiene diarrea means   The sick man has diarrhea.
_____ tiene fiebre means   The sick woman has a fever.

4.   The **suffix -ero** and **-era** (like the English suffix -er) often indicates a masculine or feminine profession, respectively. **El enferm<u>ero</u>** is a noun which means the male nurse and **la enferm<u>era</u>** is a noun which means the female nurse.

jardín means garden, jardin**ero** means gardener
mensaje means message, mensajero means _____
leche means milk, lech ___ means _____
fruta means fruit, frut ___ means _____
enfermo means sick man, enferm ___ means _____
enferma means sick woman, enferm ___ means ____

So, if you were paying attention, you would know that:

la enfermedad (remember -ity)   _____.
enfermo   _____.
enferma   _____.
el enfermo   _____.
la enferma   _____.
el enfermero   _____.
la enfermera   _____.

7.2 THE INVISIBLE PRONOUN "IT"

VOCABULARY AND STRESS GUIDE

nouns
la gar<u>gan</u>ta   the throat
el mos<u>qui</u>to   the mosquito
la pi<u>e</u>l   the skin
la <u>lla</u>ga   the sore
la flor   the fower

la a<u>xi</u>la   the axilla
el <u>flu</u>jo   the discharge
la he<u>ri</u>da   the wound
el pus   the pus

verbs
<u>que</u>ma   it burns
<u>pi</u>ca   it itches
du<u>e</u>le   it hurts
hu<u>e</u>le   it smells

Back on page 51, we learned that in Spanish, there is no subject pronoun "it." To say "it is wet," we simply said "is wet," or **está mojado**, and forgot all about the pronoun. But what if we want to say "it hurts," or "it burns"? I can't believe that you just say "hurts" and "burns!" It's just too simple! Well, I wish I could make it more difficult for you so you could complain a little, and feel justified. But I'm afraid I can't indulge you. It really is as simple as it sounds.

El dedo de Pepe está quemado, la mano de Pepe está quemada y el codo de Pepe está quemado.

El dedo quemado de Pepe quema.   **El dedo quema.**[1]
La mano quemada de Pepe quema.   **La mano quema.**
El codo quemado de Pepe quema.   **El codo quema.**

¿Quema el dedo?   Sí, el dedo quema.
¿Quema la mano?   Sí, _____.
_____ el codo?   Sí, el codo quema.
_____ el ojo?   Sí, _____.
_____ la garganta?   Sí, _____.

Translate into Spanish:
Burns the stomach after[2] you eat?   _____.
Burns the stomach before you eat?   _____.

---

[1] In this sense, **quemar** is an intransitive verb. Quemar can also be transitive, as in "yo quemo la casa" (I burn the house). All the verbs in this section will be used only as intransitive verbs.

[2] Remember, **antes de** and **después de**, being prepositions, take infinitives, i.e., **antes de orinar**; whereas **cuando**, being an adverb, needs to have the verb which follows it conjugated, i.e., **cuando yo orino**.

Burns the stomach when you eat? _____.
Burns when you eat? _____.
Burns when you urinate? _____.
Burns when you eliminate? _____.
Burns when you swallow? _____.

El mosquito pica el brazo de Juan, la pierna de Juan, y la cabeza de Juan.

El brazo de Juan pica.   **El brazo pica.**
La pierna de Juan pica.   **La pierna pica.**
La cabeza de Juan pica.   **La cabeza pica.**

¿Pica el brazo?   Sí, el brazo pica.
¿Pica la pierna?   Sí, _____.
____ la cabeza?   Sí, la cabeza pica.
____ la piel?   Sí, _____.
____ el pie?   Sí, _____.

Translate into Spanish:
Itches/stings when you urinate? _____.
Itches/stings when you eliminate? _____.
Itches/stings when you swallow? _____.

La cabeza de Pepe está hinchada, el ojo de Pepe está hinchado, y el pie de Pepe está hinchado.

La cabeza de Pepe duele.   **La cabeza duele.**
El ojo de Pepe duele.   **El ojo duele.**
El pie de Pepe duele.   **El pie duele.**

¿Duele la cabeza?   Sí, la cabeza duele.
¿Duele el ojo?   Sí, _____.
____ el pie?   Sí, el pie duele.
____ la espalda?   Sí, _____.
____ la llaga?   Sí, _____.

Translate into Spanish:
Hurts the sore on the skin? _____.
Hurts the throat? _____.
Hurts the throat when you swallow? _____.
Hurts when you urinate? _____.
Hurts when you breathe? _____.
Hurts when you eat? _____.

La flor en el jardín huele bien.   **La flor huele bien.**
El pie de Pepe huele mal.   **El pie huele mal.**
La axila de Pepe huele mal.   **La axila huele mal**.

¿Huele bien la flor?   Sí, la flor huele bien.
¿Huele mal el pie?   Sí, _____.
____ mal la axila?   Sí, la axila huele mal.
____ mal la orina?   Sí, _____.
¿Cómo huele la orina?   _____.
____ ___ el excremento?   _____.

Translate into Spanish:
What's the discharge smell like?   _____.
What's the discharge from the
   vagina smell like?   _____.
What's the discharge from the
   sore smell like?   _____.
What's the discharge from the
   wound smell like?   _____.
What's the pus smell like?   _____.
What's the pus from the
   wound smell like?   _____.

I thought you said this was going to be simple! Actually, it only *seems*
difficult .... Remembering that no pronoun before a verb implies "it," then:

quema means   __ burns
pica means   __ itches/stings
duele means   __ hurts
huele means   __ smells

and remembering that "does" does not exist in Spanish, then:

¿quema? means   ___ ___ burn?
¿pica? means   ___ ___ ___
¿duele? means   ___ ___ ___
¿huele? means   ___ ___ ___

So, if you want to say,

Does it burn? you say   _____.
Does it itch/sting? you say   _____.

Does it hurt? you say   _____.
Does it smell? you say   _____.

and to say,

Does it burn when you urinate?   _____.
Does it itch/sting when you
    swallow?   _____.
Does it hurt when you have
    sexual relations?   _____.
Does it smell when you move
    your bowels?   _____.

Simple, right?

7.3 I KNOW/I DON'T KNOW

VOCABULARY AND STRESS GUIDE

nouns

el picazón	the itching
los geni<u>ta</u>les	the genitals
la mo<u>les</u>tia	the discomfort
las <u>par</u>tes pri<u>va</u>das	the private parts (genitals)
el <u>nom</u>bre	the name
la <u>ca</u>lle	the street
el número	the number
el se<u>gu</u>ro médico	the medical insurance

Do you find yourself shrugging your shoulders, putting your hands up and lifting your eyebrows a lot with your Spanish-speaking patients? Next time, look more professional by saying: **yo no sé.** The infinitive form is **saber**. It is irregular only in the first person, yo.

SABER

yo sé	I know
usted sabe	you know
él sabe	he knows
ella sabe	she knows

Translate into Spanish:

I know.	Yo sé.
I know to speak in Spanish.	Yo sé hablar en español.
I know to speak in English.	_____.
I know to open the door.	_____.
I know to close the door.	_____.
I don't know.	Yo no sé.
I don't know to speak in Spanish.	_____.
I don't know to open the door.	_____.
Do you know?	¿Sabe usted?
Do you know to speak in English?	_____.
Do you know to take the medicament?	_____.
Do you know when to take the medicament?	_____.
Do you know when begins the pain?	_____.
Do you know what begins the pain?	_____.
Do you know when begins the itching?	_____.
Do you know when begins the itching of the genitals?	_____.
Do you know what begins the discomfort?	_____.
Do you know what begins the discomfort of the private parts?[3]	_____.
Do you know what begins the itching of the anus?	_____.
Do you know the name of your doctor?	_____.
Do you know the name of your street?	_____.
Do you know the number of your street?	_____.
Do you know the number of your medical insurance?	_____.

---

[3]"Partes privadas" is a euphemism for genitals.

7.4 PLEASE!

VOCABULARY AND STRESS GUIDE

nouns
el inodoro   the toilet
la crema   the cream

adverbs
despacio   slowly
rápido   quickly

When giving a command, we usually indicate it by our voice, our face (mostly in the brow), our index finger, and, if we're polite, by saying "please." I suggest that you use all these when giving orders in Spanish, except that instead of saying "please," say **por favor.**

By adding **por favor** at the beginning or at the end of the sentence, you make your orders polite and no matter what tense you're using, the patient will get the message that you're giving a command.

The following are all regular verbs. Notice that as in English, when giving a command, we do not say: "Please you speak more slowly," or "You, speak more slowly!" (unless you're in a Martin Scorsese movie). In Spanish, we also omit the "you."

You speak more slowly.   Usted habla _____ despacio.
Speak more slowly, please!   ¡Hable _____ por favor!
You urinate in the toilet.   Usted orina ___ el inodoro.
Urinate in the toilet, please!   ¡Orin_ _____.
Don't urinate in the toilet!   ¡No _____.

Translate into Spanish:
You breathe deep.   _____.
Breathe deep, please!   _____.
You speak quickly.   _____.
Don't speak quickly, please!   _____.
Don't urinate here, please!   _____.
Take 2 tablets each day, please!   _____.

You cough.   Usted tos**e**.
Cough, please!   ¡Tos**a**, por favor!
You eat more slowly.   Usted com**e** _____.
Eat more slowly, please!   ¡Com_ _____.

Translate into Spanish:
Drink milk, please!   _____.
Don't eat before the operation,
  please!   _____.

You open the mouth.   Usted abr**e** la boca.
Open the mouth, please!   ¡Abr**a** la boca, por favor!
You live in California.   Usted viv**e** _____.
Live in California, please!   ¡Viv_ _____.

Translate into Spanish:
Live with your mother, please!   _____.
Don't open your mouth, please!   _____.
Don't suffer, please!   _____.

The following are two verbs that have slightly irregular commands:

I have.   _____.
Have, please!   ¡Tenga, por favor!
Have the bottle, please![4]   _____.
Have the boy, please!   _____.
Don't have sexual relations before
  the treatment, please!   _____.
I put.   _____.
Put, please!   ¡Ponga, por favor!
Put the tablet under your tongue,
  please!   _____.
Don't put the cream on your lip
  before eating, please!   _____.
Don't put the cream on the skin of
  the baby, please!   _____.

---

[4]As in English, this can mean, "Take the bottle, please," or "Have the bottle with you,
please."

7.5 HOW TO WIN A FREE ROUND TRIP TICKET FOR TWO TO CANCUN

You mean that you didn't know that included in the price of this <u>Manual</u> was the chance to win a free trip to Cancún? That you could be basking in the sun, conjugating the verb cerveza? (What, you mean cerveza isn't a verb? I could have sworn ...)

Actually, there is no such contest. I'm sorry to have tricked you in such a shameless way, but how else can I get you to start reading a section devoted entirely to conjugating verbs? Certainly not by entitling it "Verb Conjugation," right?

Well, if you can't be relaxing at the beach, you can at least take off your shoes and get comfortable. Look below. You will notice (you might want to take your sunglasses off, too) three columns, headed by the verbs **tomar** (typical **-ar** verb), **beber** (representing the **-er** verbs), and **abrir** (standing in for the well known **-ir** verb "vivir," vacationing in Cancún). Under each of these words, you see **yo** (I), **él** (he), **ella** (she), **usted** (you, formal), and **¡por favor!** (please! for a command).

Under the blanks, there is a list of regular verbs. Conjugate them as I did with the key verbs. ¡Buen Viaje!

tomar			**beber**			**abrir**		
yo	él ella usted	¡por favor!	yo	él ella usted	¡por favor!	yo	él ella usted	¡por favor!

tomo toma ¡tome!	bebo bebe ¡beba!	abro abre ¡abra!
	aprendo	
cierro		
comienzo		
elimino		
	comprendo	
estoy		
hablo		
mastico		
orino		

tomar			**beber**			**abrir**		
yo	él	¡por favor!	yo	él	¡por favor!	yo	él	¡por favor!
	ella			ella			ella	
	usted			usted			usted	

		quiero		
respiro				
			sufro	
termino				
		toso		
trabajo				
trago				
			vivo	
vomito				

7.6 KEY CONCEPTS

la enfermedad
el enfermo
la enfermera
enfermo/a
¿Duele la cabeza?
No sé
¡Por favor!

Lesson 7

Inflamación pélvica e infección urinaria
(Pelvic Inflammatory Disease and Urinary Tract Infection)

(translate this out loud)	(check yourself with this)
Hello, how are you? Glad to meet you. My name is _____. What's your name?	¿Hola, qué tal? ¿Cómo está? Mucho gusto. Me llamo _____. ¿Cómo se llama usted?
You are here because you have a problem, right? What's the matter, please!	¿Usted está aquí porque tiene un problema, no? ¿Qué le pasa, por favor?
Where do you live? Do you know the name of your street? Do you have medical insurance?	¿Dónde vive? ¿Sabe usted el nombre de su calle? ¿Tiene usted seguro médico?
Do you know how to speak English? Do you have pain? Where is the pain? What's the pain like? For how long have you had the pain?	¿Sabe usted hablar inglés? ¿Tiene dolor? ¿Dónde está el dolor? ¿Cómo es el dolor? ¿Hace cuánto tiene el dolor?
Do you have fever? For how long have you had the fever? What temperature do you have?	¿Tiene fiebre? ¿Hace cuánto tiene la fiebre? ¿Qué temperatura tiene?
Does it hurt when you urinate? Does it smell when you urinate? Does it itch when you urinate?	¿Duele cuando orina? ¿Huele cuando orina? ¿Pica cuando orina?
Do you have a discharge from the vagina? Does the discharge smell bad? What's the discharge like? Is it transparent? With blood? White, pink, yellow-green, grey? Of what consistency is it? Is it dense (thick) or watery?	¿Tiene flujo de la vagina? ¿Huele mal el flujo? ¿Cómo es el flujo? ¿Es transparente? ¿Con sangre? ¿Blanco, rosado, amarillo-verde, gris? ¿De qué consistencia es? ¿Es denso o aguado?

Do you have sexual relations?	¿Tiene relaciones sexuales?
Does it hurt when you have sexual relations? Do you use contraception? What do you use?	¿Duele cuando tiene relaciones sexuales? ¿Usa usted contracepción? ¿Qué usa?
The pill? The IUD?	La píldora?¿El aparato (intrauterino)?
Diaphragm and jelly? Condoms and foam? Rhythm?	¿El diafragma y la jalea? ¿Condones y la espuma? ¿El rítmo?
Are you pregnant?	¿Está usted embarazada?
Do you have an abortion?[5]	¿Tiene un aborto?
Do you have an IUD recently?	¿Tiene un aparato recientemente?
Do you have pelvic inflammatory disease before?	¿Tiene inflamación pélvica antes?
Do you have allergy to penicillin?	¿Tiene alergia a penicilina?

I want an analysis of urine. Please, clean where you urinate with this gauze. Separate your private parts, urinate a little bit in the toilet, urinate in the glass, and urinate the rest in the toilet please.

Quiero un análisis de orina. Por favor, limpie donde orina con esta gasa. Separe las partes privadas, orine un poco en el inodoro, orine en el vaso, y orine el resto en el inodoro, por favor.

You have pelvic inflammatory disease and an infection of your urinary apparatus. PID is a disease transmitted when you have sexual relations with a person who has microorganisms (microbes) like gonococcus or chlamydia. The microbes enter your vagina and infect the tubes from your ovaries to your uterus. It is important to treat this infection because of the serious complications, especially ectopic pregnancy and infertility. Your case is not serious. The treatment is one injection and an antibiotic you take two times a day for ten days. Does your husband/boyfriend/partner have venereal disease? Does he have sores in his penis? Does he have sores in his anus, too? It is important to treat him also. You also have an infection of your urinary apparatus. It is not serious. Take these tablets. When you urinate, please clean your private parts from front to back. Please come to the clinic in three days!

Usted tiene una inflamación pélvica y una infección del aparato urinario. La inflamación pélvica es una enfermedad transmitida cuando usted tiene relaciones sexuales con una persona que tiene microbios como gonococo o

---

[5]Correctly, this is asked in the past tense; however, you will be understood by adding the words "recently" and "before."

clamidia. Los microbios entran en su vagina e infectan los tubos de los ovarios al útero. Es importante tratar esta infección por las complicaciones serias, especialmente embarazos ectópicos e infertilidad. Su caso no es serio. El tratamiento es una inyección y un antibiótico que usted toma dos veces por día por diez días. ¿Tiene su esposo/novio/pareja una enfermedad venerea? ¿Tiene él llagas en el pene? ¿Tiene él llagas en el ano también? Es importante tratar a él (tratarlo, correctly) también. Usted tiene una infección en el aparato urinario también. No es serio. Tome estas tabletas. Cuando orina, por favor limpie las partes privadas de adelante a atrás. ¡Por favor, venga a la clínica en tres días!

Now, go back to page 4 and look at the "Herpes" paragraph again. How much more can you understand?

Lesson 8. The Plural

8.1 THE PLURAL OF NOUNS

VOCABULARY AND STRESS GUIDE

nouns

la puntada	the stitch
la tarea	the task
la instrucción	the direction
la cicatriz	the scar
la mujer	the woman
la úlcera	the ulcer
la iglesia	the church
el hueso	the bone
el plan	the plan
el peso	the weight
el trabajo	the work
el documento	the document
el hombre	the man

adjectives

simple	simple
fácil	easy
difícil	difficult
ocupado/a	busy
rico/a	rich
pobre	poor

One of the many things we learned in Lesson 1 was how to pluralize articles, nouns, and adjectives. On the outside chance that you may have forgotten how to do it, let's do a quick review. Change the following words into their plural form, and, as always, pronounce out loud!

la enfermer**a** buen**a**
las enfermer**as** buen**as**

la herida inflamada   _____.
la puntada limpia   _____.
la tarea simple[1]   _____.
la tarea fácil[2]   _____.
la instrucción buena   _____.
la cicatriz[3] larga   _____.
la familia difícil   _____.
la doctora ocupada   _____.
la mujer buena   _____.
la mujer rica   _____.
la úlcera infectada   _____.
la iglesia grande   _____.

el enfermer**o** buen**o**
los enfermer**os** buen**os**

el hueso infectado   _____.
el tajo profundo   _____.
el problema[4] serio   _____.
el plan temporario   _____.
el peso bajo   _____.
el trabajo permanente   _____.
el documento largo   _____.
el baño ocupado   _____.
el hombre pobre   _____.
el país pobre   _____.

---

[1]If the word ends in **e** just add **s.**
[2]If the word ends in **l, n, r,** or **s** add **es.**
[3]If the word ends in **z,** drop the **z** and add **ces.**
[4]Many words ending in **ema/ama** (el sistema, el telegrama, el problema, el tema [theme]) are masculine.

8.2 THE PLURAL OF VERBS

VOCABULARY AND STRESS GUIDE

nouns

la línea	the line
el di<u>ne</u>ro	the money

verbs

cu<u>rar</u>	to cure
sa<u>nar</u>	to cure
levan<u>tar</u>	to lift
concen<u>trar</u>	to concentrate
pade<u>cer</u> de	to suffer from

So far, you can say I take, you take, he takes, she takes, it takes, but what about we take and they take? In English, of course, it's so simple any American can do it, right? Spanish is a bit more complicated (but only for foreigners). The only way to learn this is by rote. Following is a chart with the key verbs and their conjugations:

	TOMAR	BEBER	ABRIR
yo	tom**o**	beb**o**	abr**o**
él ella usted	tom**a**	beb**e**	abr**e**
nosotros (we)	tom**amos**	beb**emos**	abr**imos**
ellos (they, m.) ellas (they, f.) ustedes (you, pl.)	tom**an**	beb**en**	abr**en**
por favor	¡tom**e**!	¡beb**a**!	¡abr**a**!

You can either spend the next hour conjugating these verbs or reading Vector Calculus... Now, doesn't the task at hand seem a lot more pleasant?

	yo é l ella	ud	nosotros	ustedes ellos ellas	¡p.f!

_____.

(___) respirar   _____.
(to cure) curar   _____.
(to cure) sanar   _____.
(to lift) levantar _____.
(___) concentrar   _____.
(___) orinar   _____.
(___) vomitar   _____.
(___) fumar   _____.
(___) comer   _____.
(to learn) aprender _____.
padecer [5]   _____.
(___) vivir   _____.

The following verbs undergo "root" changes; verb-endings remain the same:

	yo é l ella	ud	nosotros	ustedes ellos ellas	¡p.f!

_____.

(to think) pensar	pienso	piensa	pensamos	piensan	¡piense!
(to lose) perder	pierdo				
(to sleep) dormir	duermo				
(to die) morir	muero				
(to feel) sentir	siento				
(to follow) seguir	sigo				

Translate into Spanish:
Follow the directions, please!   _____.
Follow the directions of the
   doctor, please!   _____.

_____

[5]Padecer is a common expression which means "to have a condition."
I have a condition of the heart-->Yo padezco del corazón.
You have a condition of the heart-->Usted padece del corazón.
Do you have a condition of the heart? ¿Padece usted del corazón?
Do you have a condition of the kidneys? _____ de los riñones?
Do you have a condition of the liver? _____ del hígado?
Do you have a condition of diabetes? ¿Padece usted de diabetes?
Do you have a condition of cancer? _____
Do you have a condition of hypertension? _____

Follow the black line to the
   pharmacy, please!   _____.
Do you want work?   _____.
Do you want your documents?   _____.
Do you want money?   _____.
Do you want more money?   _____.
Do you want to smoke?   _____.
Do you want to lift your leg?   _____.
Do you want to eat?   _____.
Do you want to sleep?   _____.
Do you want to die?   _____.
What do you want?   _____.
What do you think?   _____.
What do you lose?   _____.

8.3 THERE IS, THERE ARE

VOCABULARY AND STRESS GUIDE

nouns

el senador	the senator
el estado	the state
la persona	the person
el pelo/el cabello	the hair
el suicida	the person who commits suicide
el corazón	the heart

articles, indef.

un	a, m
una	a, f

interrogatives

¿Hay?	Is there? Are there?

pronoun

nada	nothing

If **el** dedo means **the** finger then **un** dedo means ___ finger, and
if **la** cabeza means **the** head, then **una** cabeza means ___ head.

Now, turn your minds to automatic pilot and **don't think, just repeat!**

Hay un presidente en los Estados Unidos.
Hay dos senadores en Oklahoma.
Hay cincuenta estados en los Estados Unidos.

¿Hay dos presidentes en
  los Estados Unidos?   No, no ____ dos presidentes.
¿Hay tres presidentes en
  los Estados Unidos?   No, no ____ tres presidentes.

¿Cuántos presidentes **hay** en
  los Estados Unidos?   _____ un presidente.
_____ senadores ___ en
  Oklahoma?   Hay dos senadores.
_____ estados ___ en
  los Estados Unidos?   Hay 50 estados.
¿Cuántas personas **hay** en
  su familia?   Hay 5 personas en mi familia.
_____ cabezas ___ en
  el cuerpo?   Hay 1 cabeza en el cuerpo.
_____?   Hay 52 semanas en un año.

¿Hay un estómago encima de
  la cabeza?   No, no hay un _____.
¿Hay un riñón encima de la cabeza?   No, _____.

¿Qué hay encima de la cabeza?   ____ pelo encima de la cabeza.
¿Qué hay debajo de la cabeza?   ____ un cuello _____.
¿___ ___ a la derecha de
  la cabeza?   Hay una oreja a la derecha de la cabeza.
¿___ ___ a la izquierda de
  la cabeza?   Hay una oreja a la izquierda de la cabeza.
¿___ ___ en la cabeza?   **¡No hay nada** en la cabeza!
¿Hay pelo encima de la cabeza?   Sí, _____.
___ cáncer en su familia?   Sí, hay cáncer en mi familia.
___ artritis _____?   Sí, hay artritis en mi familia.
___ alcoholismo _____?   No, no hay alcoholismo en mi familia.
___ suicidas _____?   No, ho hay suicidas en mi familia.
_____?   No, no hay tuberculosis en mi familia.
_____?   Sí, hay enfermedad del corazón en mi
                                                familia.

Whenever you want to ask "Is there a history of heart problems in your family?" don't. Just ask:

Is there	disease of the heart	in your family?
¿Hay	**enfermedad del corazón**	**en su familia?**

Are there	problems sexual	with your husband?
¿Hay	**problemas sexuales**	**con su esposo?**

8.4 SHOULD

VOCABULARY AND STRESS GUIDE

nouns

la libra	the pound
el colesterol	the cholesterol
el pulmón	the lung
la dieta	the diet
la sal	the salt
la grasa	the fat
el ejercicio	the exercise
el huevo	the egg

verbs

pesar	to weigh
hacer ejercicio	to exercise
deber	should
hacer	to do
seguir	to follow
caminar	to walk

adjective

primero	first

Pepe está en la clínica. ¿Por qué? Porque tiene una cita con la doctora. Él tiene muchos problemas. Primero, Pepe es gordo. Muy gordo. Pepe pesa 250 libras (lbs.). También, él tiene hipertensión (presión alta de la sangre), una úlcera en el estómago, colesterol muy alto, padece de diabetes, hay cáncer del pulmón en su familia, y no habla inglés (just your luck ...).

Doctora	**Pepe**
Pepe, **usted necesita** una dieta.	¿Por qué necesito una dieta?
_____ (Because you are muy fat)	¿Necesito una dieta estricta?
Sí, usted necesita _____.	¿Necesito comer menos?
Sí, _____.	¿Necesito perder peso?
Sí, _____.	¿Necesito hacer ejercicio?
Sí, _____.	¿Qué debo comer?
Debe comer menos y **debe** perder peso.	

Translate into Spanish:

You should eat less salt.   _____.

You should eat without salt.   _____.

You should eat less fat.   _____.

You should do more.   _____.

You should do more exercise.   _____.

You should follow a diet without
  salt.   _____.

You should not eat more than 1
  egg once a week.   _____.

You should not smoke.   _____.

You should not walk after
  the operation.   _____.

8.5 IS IT LIKE...?

VOCABULARY AND STRESS GUIDE

nouns

la puñal<u>a</u>da	the stab
la opresión	the constriction
el cal<u>am</u>bre	the cramp
la quema<u>du</u>ra	the burning
la indigestión	the indigestion

adjective

extr<u>a</u>ño   strange

interrogatives

¿Es cómo una puñalada?	Is it like a stab?
¿Es cómo una opresión?	Is it like a constriction?
¿Es cómo un calambre?	Is it like a cramp?
¿Es cómo una quemadura?	Is it like a burning pain?

Pepe tiene un dolor extraño en el pecho. Él va a la sala de emergencia con su esposa, Pepita. Pepita está muy preocupada porque Pepe no sigue las instrucciones de la doctora. Él no sigue la dieta estricta de la doctora... Pepe come sal, grasa, huevos, Twinkis...

Doctora

¿Qué tal, Pepe? ¿Cómo está?
¿Qué pasa? ¿Tiene dolor?
¿Cómo es el dolor?
¿Es cómo una puñalada?
_____ una opresión?
_____ (Is it like a cramp?)
_____ una quemadura?
Muy bien, Pepe. Probablemente
  es indigestión. No es serio.
  (Just stop eating those Twinkies!!)

Pepe

Muy mal, doctora.
Sí, tengo un dolor fuerte en el pecho.
No sé...
No, no es cómo una puñalada.
No, no es cómo una opresión.
No, no _____.
Sí, _____.

8.6 LIKE THIS

VOCABULARY AND STRESS GUIDE

nouns

la terapia física	the physical therapy

verbs

indicar	to indicate
rotar	to rotate
empujar	to push
repetir	to repeat
subir	to climb up
bajar	to climb down
apretar	to squeeze

adjective

tor<u>ci</u>do   twisted

Pepe va al hospital después del accidente de carro. En el accidente, Pepe sufre una pierna quebrada, un pie torcido, dos costillas quebradas, un hojo hinchado, un brazo cortado, y un dolor de cabeza terrible. ¡Pobre Pepe!

Dra: Pepe, ¿qué pasa? ¿Cómo está?
Pepe: ¡Hay, doctora! ¡Un accidente terrible! ¡Gracias a Dios Pepita está bien y yo estoy bien también! Unos pocos huesos quebrados, ¡pero nada más!

Después de unos meses, Pepe regresa a la doctora. Él está sano, no tiene más dolor, y los huesos están bien. Pero necesita tomar terapia física porque es difícil caminar y mover el cuerpo.

Dra: Por favor, Pepe, levante la pierna 5 centímetros, después rote el pie a la derecha 3 veces, rote el pie a la izquierda 3 veces, después empuje a un lado, después al otro lado, y después repita con la otra pierna....
Pepe: ¿¿¿¿¿QUÉ????? ¡Hable más despacio, por favor!
Dra: Leeeeevaaaanteeee laaa piiiieeernaaaa....
Pepe: Por favor, indique con su pierna cómo debo levantar mi pierna.
Dra: **Así** (and she lifts the leg to indicate how to do it).
Pepe: ¿Cómo debo rotar el pie?
Dra: Así (and _____)
Pepe: ¿Cómo debo empujar?
Dra: _____ (and she pushes to indicate how to do it)
Pepe: ¿Cómo debo repetir?
Dra: _____ (and she repeats to indicate how to do it)
Pepe: ¿Cómo debo caminar?
Dra: _____ (and she walks to indicate how to do it)
Pepe: ¿Cómo debo subir?
Dra: _____ (and she climbs to indicate how to do it)
Pepe: ¿Cómo debo bajar?
Dra: _____ (and she descends to indicate how to do it)
Pepe: ¿Cómo debo apretar?
Dra: _____ (and she squeezes to indicate how to do it)

Whenever you're having a hard time explaining something, try doing it (if possible) and saying: **Así.**

8.7 FROM ... UNTIL ...

VOCABULARY AND STRESS GUIDE

nouns

el desayuno	the breakfast
el almuerzo	the lunch
la cena	the dinner
el exámen	the exam
el exámen pélvico	the pelvic exam
el ataque	the attack
los nervios	the nerves
la depresión	the depression
la ansiedad	the anxiety
la desesperación	the hopelessness
la tristeza	the sadness

verbs

durar	to last

prepositions

desde	from
hasta	until

El desayuno comienza a las 7 de la mañana.
El desayuno termina a las 7:30 de la mañana.
Yo como **desde** las 7 **hasta** las 7:30.

El almuerzo comienza a las 12.
El almuerzo termina a la 1.
Yo como _____ las 12 _____ la 1.

¿A qué hora comienza el desayuno?　_____ a las 7 de la mañana.

¿A qué hora termina el desayuno?　_____ a las 7:30 de la mañana.

El desayuno **dura** 30 minutos.
¿A qué hora comienza el almuerzo?　_____.
¿A qué hora termina el almuerzo?　_____.

El almuerzo ___ una hora.
¿El desayuno dura 12 horas?   No, _____.
¿El desayuno dura 11 horas?   No, _____.
¿Cuánto tiempo dura el
   desayuno?   _____.
¿Cuánto tiempo dura el almuerzo?   _____.
_____ _____ dura la cena?   _____.
_____ _____ dura el examen?   _____.
_____ _____ ___ el examen
   pélvico?   _____.
_____ _____ ___ el ataque?   _____.

Translate into Spanish:
How long does the attack of
   nerves last?   _____.
How long does the depression last?   _____.
How long does the anxiety last?   _____.
How long does the hopelessness
   last?   _____.
How long does the sadness last?   _____.

8.8 TOO MUCH/TOO, NOT ENOUGH

VOCABULARY AND STRESS GUIDE

nouns
la caloría   the calorie
el paquete de cigarrillos   the packet of cigarettes

adjectives
demasiado/a   too much
no suficiente   not enough

adverb
sólo   only
demasiado   too

¡Pepe come 4,000 calorías por día!
¡Pepe come **demasiado**!
¡Pepe duerme 14 horas por día!

Pepe duerme _____.
¡Pepe fuma 2 paquetes de cigarrillos por día!
Pepe _____ _____.
¡Pepe sólo trabaja media hora por día!
¡Pepe **no** trabaja **suficiente**!

On the other hand...

Juan come sólo 500 calorías por día...
Juan no come suficiente.
Juan duerme sólo 3 horas por día...
Juan ____ duerme _____.
Juan hace ejercicio una vez por año...
Juan ____ hace ejercicio _____.
Juan trabaja 18 horas por día...
Juan _____.
(Is Juan an intern??)

¡¡La presión de Juan es 200/130!!!!
La presión está demasiado alta.
La presión de Pepe es 70/40....
La presión está _____ baja.
¡El pulso de Juan es 150!
El pulso está _____ _____.
El pulso de Pepe es 20...
El pulso está _____ _____.

After giving Juan and Pepe the appropriate medication, you realize that
the above section has you quite confused. Are you telling me that
demasiado is "too much" and that **demasiado grande** is "too big"? So
why isn't demasiado pequeño, "too much small"? Well, if that's how you
want to start speaking English, that's fine by me (there will be a sequel to
this textbook, *How to Communicate in English with Your Family and
Friends*, which you might consider buying).

8.9 INSIDE, OUTSIDE

VOCABULARY AND STRESS GUIDE

nouns

la muerte   the death

adjectives

empleado/a   employed
casado/a   married

prepositions

en   inside/in
fuera de   outside of

Just remember that la lengua está **en** la boca and that el dedo está **fuera de** la nariz, and you'll do just fine.

Translate into Spanish:
Is the pain in the head?   _____.
Is the burning in the eye?   _____.
Is the death outside of the family? _____.
Is the suicide in the family?   _____.
Are the men employed outside of
   the country?   _____.
Does[6] your married sister live in
   the house with you?   _____.

8.10 PARA VS POR

VOCABULARY AND STRESS GUIDE

nouns

el potasio   the potassium
la salud   the health
el amigo   the friend, m

---

[6]As always, forget about "does" when speaking Spanish, it does not exist, and cannot be translated! This sentence should be translated as: "Your sister married lives inside the house with you?"

la a<u>mi</u>ga   the friend, f

verb
qui<u>tar</u>   to take away

prepositions
por   see text
<u>pa</u>ra   see text

demonstrative pronouns
<u>es</u>ta   this, f
<u>es</u>tas   these, f
<u>es</u>te   this, m
<u>es</u>tos   these, m

Just repeat after me, and avoid thinking:
This tableta is for the pain.
Esta _____ __ para __ _____.
This tablet is for the diarrhea.

_____.

These tablets are for the pain.
Estas _____ son ___ __ _____.
These tablets are for the fever.

_____.

For what are these tablets?

_____.

These tablets are for taking away the pain.
_____ **quitar** _____.
These tablets are for taking away the diarrhea.

_____.

These tablets are for taking away the depression.

_____.

These tablets are for taking away the water.

_____.

These tablets are for lowering your blood pressure.
_____ **bajar** _____.
These tablets are for lowering your cholesterol.

_____.

These tablets are for raising the iron in the blood.
_____ **subir** _____.
These tablets are for raising your potassium.
_____ potasio.

Note that after the preposition **para**, the verb following is always in the infinitive (-ar, -er, or -ir form).

Translate into Spanish (speaking to a woman):

Are you?	_____?
Are you worried (remember preoccupied ...)?	_____?
Are you worried **about** the money?	_____ por_____?
Are you worried about your health?	_____?
Are you worried about the health of your spouse?	_____?
Are you worried about the entertainment (also: fun)?	_____?

Some of you might make the mistake of thinking that because "for" and **por** sound similar, they mean the same thing. They don't. **Por** means "through," "along," "by," "around," "by" (passive), "per," "to go for," "for" in the expression of time only, and "about" as in the expression above. Aren't you glad you asked? So, if you want to say "for," think **para**. And if you want to say anything else, think **por.** (Typical sentence might therefore sound like: "por por por para por por?)

8.11 BUILD YOUR OWN EXPRESSIONS

The difficulty	_____.
Difficulty	_____.
Difficulty in taking (to take)	_____ en tomar.
Difficulty in taking decisions	_____ decisiones.
Difficulty in taking difficult decisions	_____.
Difficulty in working (to work)	_____.
Difficulty in thinking (to think)	_____.
Difficulty in sleeping (to sleep)	_____.
Difficulty in concentrating (to concentrate)	_____.

8.12 KEY CONCEPTS

el doctor ocupado/ la doctora ocupada
el enfermero ocupado/ la enfermera ocupada
¿Hay enfermedad del corazón en su familia?
No debe fumar
Así
¿Cuánto tiempo dura el ataque?

Lesson 8

La depresión
(Depression)

(translate this out loud)   **(check yourself with this)**

Hello. My name is ____
What's your name?

Hola. Me llamo ____
¿Cómo se llama usted?

How are you?
From what country do you come?
Do you speak English?
What does your family
  speak in your house?
Do your children speak English?

¿Cómo está usted?
¿De qué país viene usted?
¿Habla usted inglés?
¿Qué habla su familia
  en su casa?
¿Hablan sus hijos inglés?

Are you married?
Do you have children?
Do you live with your family?
For how long have you been living
  in the United States?
Where is the rest of
  your family?
Do you have documents?

¿Está casada?
¿Tiene hijos?
¿Vive con su familia?
¿Hace cuánto vive
  en los Estados Unidos?
¿Dónde está el resto de
  su familia?
¿Tiene documentos?

Are there problems in your house?
Are there problems with your
  husband? With your children?

¿Hay problemas en su casa?
¿Hay problemas con su
  esposo/marido? ¿Con sus hijos?

Are you worried about your family
  here? About your family in ____?
Are you worried about money?
About your documents?
About your health?

¿Está preocupada por su familia
  aquí? ¿Por su familia en ___?
¿Está preocupada por dinero?
¿Por sus documentos?
¿Por su salud?

Do you have work?
Where do you work?
Is the work temporary
  or permanent? Do you have enough

¿Tiene trabajo?
¿Dónde trabaja?
¿Es el trabajo temporario
  o permanente? ¿Tiene suficiente

money? Enough work?

Are you happy with your work?

Do you work less than before?

Do you have friends? Do you have fewer friends than before?

Do you go to church? Do you go to church less than before?

Do you have activities?

What do you do to relax? What do you do for entertainment (fun)?

Are you sad much? Do you have anxiety? Hopelessness?

Are you depressed? Tired?

Do you eat well? Do you eat less?

Do you lose weight?[8] How much do you lose? Do you eat more?

Do you have difficulty in sleeping?

Do you sleep more or less?

Do you have sexual relations with your spouse?

Do you have fewer sexual relations with your spouse than before?

Do you have difficulty in thinking? Concentrating?

Working? Taking decisions?

Do you think on death?

Do you think on suicide?

Are there suicides in your family?

Who? Do you have a plan?

What is it?

You think of suicide before?

---

dinero? ¿Suficiente trabajo?

¿Está contenta con su trabajo?

¿Trabaja menos que antes?

¿Tiene amigos?

¿Tiene menos amigos que antes?

¿Va a una iglesia? ¿Va a la iglesia menos que antes?

¿Tiene actividades?

¿Qué hace para relajar?[7]

¿Qué hace para entretenimiento?

¿Está triste mucho? ¿Tiene ansiedad? ¿Desesperación?

¿Está deprimida? ¿Cansada?

¿Come bien? ¿Come menos?

¿Usted pierde peso? ¿Cuánto peso pierde usted? ¿Come más?

¿Tiene dificultad en dormir?

¿Duerme usted más o menos?

¿Tiene usted relaciones sexuales con su esposo?

¿Tiene menos relaciones sexuales con su esposo que antes?

¿Tiene dificultad en pensar? ¿En concentrar?

¿En trabajar? ¿En tomar decisiones?

¿Piensa usted en la muerte?

¿Piensa usted en el suicidio? ¿Hay

¿Hay suicidas en su familia?

¿Quién? ¿Tiene usted un plan?

¿Qué es?

¿Usted piensa en el suicidio antes?

---

[7]Most correctly: "Qué hace para relajar**se**?" To relax is a reflexive verb. More on these verbs in Lesson 12. If you say it as in the text above, you will be understood.

[8]Many of the following questions should be asked in the past tense; however, you will be understood if you ask these questions in the present tense.

Lesson 9. The Preterit

9.1 THE PRETERIT

VOCABULARY AND STRESS GUIDE

nouns

la pu<u>e</u>rta	the door
el periódico	the newspaper
la vent<u>a</u>na	the window
el pa<u>sa</u>do	the past
the preterit	the past

verbs

gri<u>tar</u>	to scream
lla<u>mar</u> a	to call to
pregun<u>tar</u> a	to ask of
sen<u>tir</u>	to feel
estornu<u>dar</u>	to sneeze
cau<u>sar</u>	to cause
dor<u>mir</u>	to sleep
sa<u>lir</u>	to leave

adjective

próximo	next

adverbs

hoy	today
a<u>yer</u>	yesterday
ma<u>ñ</u>ana	tomorrow

Pepe está en su casa. Él vive con Pepita. Juan vive en otra casa, al lado de la casa de Pepe y Pepita. Hoy Pepe va a la puerta de su casa y abre la puerta. Juan está fuera de su casa y habla con Pepe cuando Pepe abre su puerta. Ellos hablan unos minutos y después Juan regresa a su casa. El periódico está fuera de la casa, encima del piso, delante de la puerta de Pepe. Pepe toma el periódico, pero en ese instante, ¡auuuuuu!, Pepe siente un dolor fuertísimo en su espalda. Pepe grita "¡¡¡AAAAAAUUUUUUU!!!" y cierra la puerta. Pepe respira profundo. "¡¡¡AAAAUUUUU!!!" grita Pepe otra vez. Después Pepe llama a Pepita, su esposa: "¡¡¡Pepitaaaaaaaaa!!!"

Ese día, Pepita está muy preocupada por Pepe, pero Pepe (being the macho-man that he is) no va a la doctora. Él va a la doctora el próximo día. Él va a la doctora mañana. El próximo día en el hospital, la doctora pregunta a Pepe:

Doctora	**Pepe**
Pepe, **¿qué pasó ayer?**	
¿Fue usted a la cama ayer?	No, doctora, no **fui** a la cama ayer.
__ usted a la casa de su tío ayer?	No, no fui a la casa de mi tío ayer.
¿Adónde fue usted ayer?	Ayer fui a la puerta.
¿Abrió usted la ventana ayer?	No, no abrí la ventana ayer.
_____ el garage ayer?	No, no abrí el garage ayer.
¿Qué _____ ayer?	Ayer yo abrí la puerta.
¿Habló usted con Ramón ayer?	No, no hablé con Ramón ayer.
_____ con Marcos ayer?	No, no hablé con Marcos ayer.
¿Con quién _____ ayer?	Ayer yo hablé con Juan.
¿Tomó usted la botella ayer?	No, no tomé la botella ayer.
_____ la venda ayer?	No, no tomé la venda ayer.
¿Qué ____ ayer?	Ayer yo tomé el periódico.
¿Gritó Pepita ayer?	No, Pepita no _____ ayer.
_____ Juan ayer?	No, Juan no gritó ayer.
¿Quién _____ ayer?	Yo grité ayer.

Y después, ¿usted _____ó? (breathed)?
Y después, ¿usted _____? (closed the door)?
Y después, ¿usted _____? (called to Pepita)?
Y después, ¿usted **sintió** ___? (felt a pain)?
Y después, ¿usted _____? (felt a pain in the back)?

Congratulations, you have just learned the past tense in Spanish. Following is a table with key verbs in the **past tense** (preterit).

	TOMAR	**BEBER** **ABRIR**
yo	tom**é**	beb }**í** abr
él ella } usted	tom**ó**	beb }**i ó** abr

¿Trabajó usted ayer?   Sí, yo **trabajé** ayer.
¿Fumó usted ayer?   Sí, yo _____**é** ayer.
¿Respiró usted ayer?   Sí, yo _____ ayer.
¿Habló usted ayer?   Sí, _____.
¿Vomitó usted ayer?   Sí, _____.
¿Estornudó usted ayer?   Sí, _____.
¿Causó un accidente ayer?   Sí, _____.

¿Comió usted ayer?   Sí, yo **comí** ayer.
¿Bebió usted ayer?   Sí, yo _____**í** ayer.
¿Tosió usted ayer?   Sí, yo _____ ayer.
¿Aprendió usted ayer?   Sí, _____.
¿Perdió usted ayer?   Sí, _____.

¿Abrió usted ayer?   Sí, yo **abrí** ayer.
¿Vivió usted ayer?   Sí, yo _____**í** ayer.
¿Sufrió usted ayer?   Sí, _____.
¿Siguió usted ayer?   Sí, _____.
¿Durmió usted ayer?   Sí, _____.
¿Salió usted ayer?   Sí, _____.

By now your head is swimming in these ridiculous endings; you're having a hard enough time remembering the -ar verbs in the present, let alone the -er and -ir verbs, and now you expect me to learn all these verbs again, but in the past???? Give me a break! O.K., O.K. Here's your break: try to remember the preterit endings

	-AR	**-ER/-IR**
yo	**-e**	**-í**
usted	**-ó**	**-i ó**

but if you can't, and its imperative that you communicate something in the past tense to your patient (i.e., "did you urinate" instead of "are you urinating?"), then just remember how to say:

YESTERDAY = AYER
IN THE PAST = EN EL PASADO

These next statements sound horrible and are absolutely incorrect, but understandable nevertheless:

¿Toma su medicamento **ayer**? (correct: ¿Tomó su medicamento ayer?)
¿Tiene vómitos **en el pasado**? (correct: ¿Tuvo vómitos en el pasado?)

9.2 THE PRETERIT OF "TO BE" (SER) AND "TO GO" (IR)

VOCABULARY AND STRESS GUIDE

adverb
a<u>ho</u>ra   now

One last word on the past. The past of the verb **ser** (to be) is the same as the past of the verb **ir** (to go).

	PRESENTE		PASADO
	SER	IR	SER/IR
yo	soy	voy	fui
él ella usted	es	va	fue
nosotros	somos	vamos	fuimos
ellos ellas ustedes	son	van	fueron

The days of the week are good to memorize:

lunes	Monday
martes	Tuesday
miércoles	Wednesday
jueves	Thursday
viernes	Friday
sábado	Saturday
domingo	Sunday

Hoy **es** lunes.
Ayer **fue** domingo.
Hoy __ martes.
Ayer ___ lunes.
Hoy __ miércoles.
Ayer ___ _____.
Hoy __ jueves.
Ayer ___ _____.
Hoy __ viernes.
Ayer ___ _____.
Hoy __ sábado.
Ayer ___ _____.
Hoy __ domingo.
Ayer ___ _____.
Hoy __ lunes.
Ayer ___ _____.

Ahora Pepe **va a** la puerta.
Ayer, Pepe **fue a** la puerta.
Ahora, Pepe __ __ la ventana.
Ayer, Pepe ___ __ la ventana.
_____, Pepe va a la casa de Juan.
_____, Pepe fue a la casa de Juan.

9.3 THE PRETERIT OF "TO BE" (ESTAR)

VOCABULARY AND STRESS GUIDE

nouns

la escuela	the school
la cárcel	the prison
el aire contaminado	the pollution
el humo	the smoke

adjective

pasado/a	past/last

ESTAR

	PRESENTE	**PASADO**
yo	estoy	estuve
él ella usted	está	estuvo
nosotros	estamos	estuvimos
ellos ellas ustedes	están	estuvieron

Dra: Pepe, ¿dónde está Pepita ahora?
Pepe: Pepita está en la casa.
Dra: ¿**Estuvo** Pepita en la escuela ayer?
Pepe: Sí, Pepita _____ en la escuela ayer.
Dra: ¿Estuvo Pepita en la clínica ayer?
Pepe: Sí, Pepita _____.
Dra: ¿**Estuvo usted** en la escuela ayer?
Pepe: Sí, yo estuve en la escuela ayer.
Dra: _____ en Hawaii ayer?
Pepe: No, yo no estuve en Hawaii ayer.
Dra: _____ en Tahiti el mes pasado?
Pepe: No, yo no estuve en Tahiti el mes pasado.

Translate into Spanish:
Were you in the hospital last year?   _____.
Were you in prison last month?   _____.
Were you in a country with
  pollution[1] (contaminated air)?   _____.
Were you in a room with smoke?   _____.

9.4 THE PRETERIT OF "TO HAVE" (TENER)

VOCABULARY AND STRESS GUIDE

nouns

los escalofríos	the chills
el resfrío	the cold

---

[1] Beware! "Polución" means "ejaculate." This is not the time to invent!!

la emoción   the emotion

TENER
	PRESENTE	**PASADO**
yo	tengo	tuve
él ella usted	tiene	tuvo
nosotros	tenemos	tuvimos
ellos ellas ustedes	tienen	tuvieron

Dra: **¿Tuvo** Pepita diarrea ayer?
Pepe: ¡Sí ella **tuvo** muuuuuucha diarrea!!
Dra: **¿Tuvo** Pepita escalofríos ayer?
Pepe: Sí, _____.
Dra: **¿Tuvo usted** un accidente?
Pepe: Sí, **yo tuve** _____.
Dra: _____ un resfrío la semana pasada?
Pepe: Sí, yo tuve un resfrío la semana pasada.
Dra: _____ emociones fuertes ayer?
Pepe: Sí, yo tuve emociones fuertes ayer.

9.5 THAT

VOCABULARY AND STRESS GUIDE

nouns
la voz   the voice
el asma   the asthma
el gato   the cat
el perro   the dog
el animal   the animal

adjective
tímido/a   timid

conjunction
que   that

En la clínica de pediatría, su paciente es un niño muy joven y muy tímido. Él habla en voz muy baja, y usted no comprende cuando él habla. La madre del paciente está al lado de él. Usted pregunta al paciente:

Dra: _____? (Do you[2] have pain of the stomach?)
Niño: BSHBSHBSHBSHBSHBSHBSH......
Dra: _____? (Please, ma'am, what says the child?)
Madre: El niño dice **que** tiene dolor de estómago.
Dra: _____? (Do you have diarrhea?)
Niño: BSHBSHBSHBSHBSHBSHBSH....
Madre: El niño dice _____ tiene diarrea.
El niño dice _____ tiene náusea.
El niño dice _____ tiene asma.
El niño dice _____ tiene un gato en la casa.
El niño dice _____ tiene un perro en la casa.
El niño dice _____ tiene muchos animales en la casa.
El niño dice _____ hace ejercicio.
El niño dice _____ no hace ejercicio.

Qué in Spanish means "what"-- **que** means "that." It's all in the accent.

9.6 ORDINAL NUMBERS

VOCABULARY AND STRESS GUIDE

nouns
el piso	the floor
la farmacia	the pharmacy
la cafetería	the cafeteria
el departamento	the department
cardiología	cardiology
psiquiatría	psychiatry
la sala de cuidado intensivo	the intensive care unit

ordinal numbers
primer	first
segundo	second

---

[2]Even though you're speaking to a child and would normally use the informal "tú," you only know the formal "usted" so go ahead and use the form you know.

ter<u>ce</u>r	third
cu<u>a</u>rto	fourth
<u>qui</u>nto	fifth
<u>sex</u>to	sixth

adjective

último/a	last

psiquiatría	**último piso**
pediatría	**sexto piso**
cardiología	**quinto piso**
cuidado intensivo	**cuarto piso**
cirugía	**tercer piso**
la cafetería	**segundo piso**
la farmacia	**primer piso**

¿Dónde está la farmacia?   _____.

¿Dónde está la cafetería?   _____.

¿Dónde está el departamento
de cirugía?   _____.

¿Dónde está la sala de
cuidado intensivo?   _____.

¿Dónde está el departamento
de cardiología?   _____.

¿Dónde está el departamento
de pediatría?   _____.

¿Dónde está el departamento
de psiquiatría?   _____.

9.7 PUTTING THE PIECES TOGETHER

Now, for some heavy-duty building. Translate only the phrases in **bold**:

Do you have diarrhea?   _____.

For how long do you have diarrhea?   _____.

The pharmacy is on the **first** floor.   _____.

The baby takes vitamins one **time** per day   _____.

The boy says **that** he has a cat.   _____.

Did you have an accident?   _____.

Does it hurt **when** you urinate?   _____.
Today is Monday; yesterday **was** Sunday.   _____.
The department of psychiatry is on the **last** floor.   _____.

Now you're ready for:

Do you have diarrhea?   _____.
For how long do you have diarrhea?   _____.
Is (this) **the first time that** you have diarrhea?   _____.
When was the last time that you **had** diarrhea?_____.

Do you breathe with wheezes?   _____ silbidos?
For how long do you breathe
   with wheezes?   _____.
Is this the first time that you
   breathe with wheezes?   _____.
When was the last time that you
   breathed with wheezes?   _____.

Do you take medicaments?   _____.
For how long do you take
   medicaments?   _____.
Is this the first time that you take
   medicaments?   _____.
When was the last time that you
   took medicaments?   _____.

Are you pregnant?   _____.
For how long are you pregnant?   _____.
Is this the first time that you are
   pregnant?   _____.
When was the last time that you
   were pregnant?   _____.

Don't despair if you couldn't ask all the questions above in Spanish. You can approach Spanish in two ways. One is by building with new blocks upon foundations you already know. For example, to ask, **"When was the last time that you took heroin?"** you need to put some new blocks on foundations that you already know: **When** opens the pharmacy?; Yesterday **was** Monday; The psychiatry department is on the **last** floor; The baby takes vitamins one **time** per day; The child says **that** he has diarrhea; Pepe **took** the newspaper yesterday; and **heroin**, for which you will have to resort to your own creative genius.

Translating you come up with: **¿Cuándo** abre la farmacia?; Ayer **fue** lunes; El departamento de psiquiatría está en el **último** piso; El bebe toma vitaminas una **vez** por día; El niño dice **que** tiene diarrea; Pepe **tomó** el periódico ayer; **heroína.** Putting them one on top of the other, we get (or at least I do): **¿Cuándo fue la última vez que tomó heroína?** Whew! All that work just to ask <u>one</u> measley question?

The second approach is to memorize all the answers by rote. I think that the building block method is funner and more instructive, but then, I already know Spanish, so who am I to talk?

9.8 COGNATES, YIPPEEEE!

Remember cognates? No, they're not the little animals that make their homes in tide pools; they are similar-sounding words in English and Spanish, the reason why you started to learn Spanish in the first place, right? It just seems like we haven't seen enough of them so far, doesn't it? Well, here's a list of some words that will come in handy in the following interview.

Nouns that end in -tion change to -ción and are always feminine
stimulation
injection
respiration
medication
emotion

Words that begin with sp- or st- change to begin with esp- or est-
spontaneous
special
Spanish (kind of)
spasm
spectacular
speculum
sperm
stable
stomach
stupid

Adverbs change -ly to -mente
progressively
immediately
specially
rapidly

Some verbs: add -ar usually, infrequently -er or -ir
permit
occur
stimulate
cause
obstruct
escape
dilate
conduct

Some nouns: add el or la to the front and -a or -o to the end
vein
oxygen
mask
animals
tube

Some adjectives: add -a or -o to the end
common
rapid
humid
reactive

9.9 KEY CONCEPTS

Ayer
En el pasado
¿Tiene X?
¿Hace cuánto tiene X?
¿Es la primera vez que tiene X?
¿Cuándo fue la última vez que tuvo X?

Lesson 9

El niño con asma
(The Child with Asthma)

(translate this out loud)   **(check yourself with this)**

(Speaking with the mother of a six-year-old boy)

Hello! How are you? My name is _____ I am the pediatrician/pediatric nurse/ medical/nursing student.	¡Hola! ¿Cómo está? Me llamo _____. Soy el pediatra/ la enfermera de pediatría/ el estudiante de medicina/ de enfermería.
Your name is Mrs. _____? And the boy's name is ___?	¿Se llama usted Señora ___? ¿Y el niño se llama _____?
How is _____ today? How was ___ yesterday?	¿Cómo está _____ hoy? ¿Cómo estuvo _____ ayer?
Does ___ have a cold? Does ___ have a cough? Does he sneeze? Does he have sputum? Does he wheeze? Does he breathe fast? Does he have difficulty with the respiration? Does he have a stomach ache? Does he have vomiting?	¿Tiene _____ un resfrío? ¿Tiene ___ tos? ¿Estornuda él? ¿Tiene esputo? ¿Respira con silbidos? ¿Respira rápido? ¿Tiene dificultad con la respiración? ¿Tiene dolor de estómago? ¿Tiene vómitos?
For how long has he been wheezing? Is this the first time that he wheezes? When was the last time that he wheezed?	¿Hace cuánto respira con silbidos? ¿Es la primera vez que él respira con silbidos? ¿Cuando fue la última vez que él respiró con silbidos?
Does he have asthma? Was he in the hospital before? Was he in the	¿Tiene asma? ¿Estuvo él en el hospital antes? ¿Estuvo él en el

hospital for his asthma?	hospital por el asma?
Was he in the intesive care unit? Was he intubated (mechanical ventilator)?	¿Estuvo él en cuidado intensivo? ¿Con el ventilador mecánico?
When was the last time that he was in the hospital?	¿Cuándo fue la última vez que estuvo en el hospital?
Is there asthma in the family?	¿Hay asma en la familia?
Who has asthma?	¿Quién tiene asma?
Do you smoke?	¿Fuma usted?
Does your husband smoke?	¿Fuma su esposo?
Is there a person at home who smokes?	¿Hay una persona en la casa que fuma?
Do you have a dog or a cat? Are there other animals in the house?	¿Tiene usted un perro o un gato? ¿Hay otros animales en la casa?
Do you work? What do you do in your work?	¿Trabaja usted? ¿Qué hace en el trabajo?
Does your husband work?	¿Trabaja su esposo?
What does your husband do in his work?	¿Qué hace su esposo en su trabajo?
Does your child take medications? What is the name of the medication?	¿Toma su hijo medicamentos? ¿Cómo se llama el medicamento?
Is the medication called Theophylline?	¿El medicamento se llama Teofilina?
Did he take any Theophylline today?	¿Tomó él Teofilina hoy?
How much did he take today?	¿Cuánto tomó él hoy?
When did he take the medication?	¿Cuándo tomó él el medicamento?
When was the last time that he took an aerosol?	¿Cuándo fue la última vez que tomó un aerosol?

(Try the following translation. Any words you don't know you can invent!)

Your child has asthma. Asthma is a very common illness in children. It is a disease of the lungs that doesn't permit air to exit. This occurs especially with stimulation like cold, exercise, smoke, pollution, and strong emotions.

The treatment for asthma is not to do the things that cause an attack. The air should be humid. Do you have a humidifier at home? It is important not to smoke.

I think that today, the treatment for ____ is oxygen with a mask. Is this the first time that ___ uses oxygen and mask?
Then (after) an aerosol that permits the air to exit from the lungs. I don't think that Aminophylline is necessary. Aminophylline is like the Theophylline that he takes in his mouth, but he takes it in his vein. Do you have questions?

Su hijo tiene asma. Asma es una enfermedad muy común en niños. Es una enfermedad de los pulmones que no permite salir el aire. Esto ocurre especialmente con el frío, con el ejercicio, con el humo, con el aire contaminado, y con emociones fuertes. El tratamiento para el asma es no hacer las cosas que causan el ataque. El aire debe estar húmedo. ¿Tiene usted un humedecedor en su casa? Es importante no fumar.

Yo creo que hoy, el tratamiento para ____ es oxígeno con una máscara. ¿Es esta la primera vez que ___ usa oxígeno y máscara? Después, un aerosol que permite salir el aire de los pulmones. No creo que Aminofilina es ("sea" instead of "es," most correctly) necesario. Aminofilina es como la Teofilina que él toma por boca, pero la toma en la vena. ¿Tiene preguntas?

Now, go back to page 4 and look at the "Herpes" paragraph again. How much more can you understand?

Lesson 10. The Verb "To Give"

10.1 THE IMPERSONAL PRONOUN

VOCABULARY AND STRESS GUIDE

nouns

la <u>sa</u>la de emer<u>gen</u>cia	the emergency room
la <u>sa</u>la de <u>par</u>tos	the labor and delivery room
el ape<u>lli</u>do	the surname/last name

verbs

co<u>rrer</u>	to run
de<u>cir</u>	to say
escri<u>bir</u>	to write

In English, whenever you want to say something unpleasant to someone who's bigger and stronger than you, such as, "One doesn't normally smoke in this elevator," you use the impersonal. You can also make a general statement, such as, "Smoking isn't allowed," and you can still consider yourself safe. If you run fast, or enjoy risking your life, you can say something like "Your smoking really disgusts me, you know." You could say this in any of the three ways and still consider yourself safe if you said them in Spanish (unless, of course, the person you were insulting spoke Spanish). You really only need to know one new word, "one" which is **se.**

One smokes in the private room.
Se ____ __ __ _____ ____
One doesn't smoke in the private room.
No se ____ __ __ _____ ____

Translate into Spanish:

One speaks Spanish in Mexico. _____.

One introduces a catheter in
the arm. (Invent!) _____.

One doesn't smoke in the E.R. _____.

One doesn't smoke in the
delivery room. _____.

One doesn't smoke in the
intensive care unit. _____.

One doesn't run here. _____.

How one says "kidneys" in Spanish?

___ __ **dice** _____ __ _____

Translate into Spanish:

How does[1] one say liver in Spanish? _____.

How does one write your name? _____.

How does one write your last name? _____.

10.2 IF

VOCABULARY AND STRESS GUIDE

nouns

el análisis   the analysis

adjectives

posi_ti_vo/a   positive

nega_ti_vo/a   negative

conjunction

si   if

Pepe: ¿Está Paul Newman en Los Angeles ahora?
Juan: No sé **si** Paul Newman está en Los Angeles ahora.
Pepe: ¿Está Al Pacino en Nueva York ahora?
Juan: No sé __ Al Pacino está en Nueva York ahora.
Pepe: ¿Está Dustin Hoffman en San Francisco ahora?
Juan: No sé __ Dustin Hoffman está en San Francisco ahora.

---

[1]Remember, "does" does not exist!

Pepe: ¿Está embarazada Pepita?
Dr: No sé __ Pepita está embarazada.
Pepe: ¿Es el análisis positivo?
Dr: No sé _____.
Pepe: ¿Es el análisis negativo?
Dr: No sé _____.

Sí in Spanish means "yes" -- **si** means if. It's all in the accent (like ¿qué? and que ... remember?)

10.3 OTHER USES OF THE VERB "TO HAVE" (TENER)

VOCABULARY AND STRESS GUIDE

nouns

los escalofríos	the chills
la al<u>er</u>gia	the allergy
el frío	the cold
el ca<u>lor</u>	the heat
el mi<u>e</u>do	the fear
la sed	the thirst
el <u>ham</u>bre	the hunger
el esófago	the esophagus

indefinite pronouns

<u>al</u>go	something
<u>na</u>da	nothing

expressions

¿Cuántos años ti<u>e</u>ne...?	How old is/are...?

In Spanish, we **have** cold, hot, hunger, thirst, fear and years. Don't say "Are you cold?" (**¿Es fría**?) unless you want to ask "Are you frigid?" or (**¿Está fría**?) unless you've just taken the patient out of the fridge and want to know if she's cold to the touch.

Translate into Spanish:
Do you have?   _____.
Do you have diarrhea?   _____.

Do you have indigestion?   _____.
Do you have chills?   _____.
Do you have allergy to aspirin?   _____ alergia a _____.
Do you have allergy to penicillin?   _____.
Do you have allergy to milk?   _____.
Do you have cold? (Are you cold?)   _____.
Do you have hotness? (Are you hot?) _____.
Do you have fear? (Are you afraid?) _____.
Do you have thirst? (Are you
    thirsty?)   _____.
Do you have hunger? (Are you
    hungry?)   _____.
How many years do you have?
    (How old are you?)   ¿Cuántos años _____?
How many years does the girl have?
    (How old is the girl?)   _____?
How many years do your parents
    have? (How old are your parents?) _____.

Do you have something?   _____ **algo?**
Do you have something in your eye?   _____.
No, no tengo **nada** en el ojo.
No, no tengo _____ en la mano.
No, no _____ _____ en el esófago.

Note the use of the double negative in Spanish. We want to make sure we're getting our point across so we say "no" three times in one sentence: **No, no** tengo **nada** en la cabeza.

10.4 FREQUENCY

VOCABULARY AND STRESS GUIDE

nouns
la comida   the meal/food
la frecuencia   the frequency
la angina   the angina
la milla   the mile
la vida   the life

verbs

pa<u>sar</u> por   to pass through
escupir   to spit

adverbs

si<u>em</u>pre   always
a me<u>nu</u>do   frequently
<u>nun</u>ca   never

adjective

<u>mu</u>cho/a   much
<u>ca</u>da   each

Didn't it seem like we just went over the una vez dos veces business a little too quickly? Well, let's review.

Pepe mueve el vientre **una vez** por día.
¿Cuántas veces mueve usted el
  vientre por día?   _____.

Pepe orina **8 veces** por día.
¿Cuántas veces orina usted por día?   _____.

Cuando Pepe orina, él orina en el inodoro.
¿Dónde orina Pepe?   _____.
¿Orina Pepe en el inodoro **siempre?** _____.
¿Orina usted en el inodoro siempre? _____.

Pepe pasa por la cafetería 15 veces por día.
Él pasa por la cafetería **muchas veces** por día.
¿Cuántas veces orina usted por mes?   _____.

Pepe come una comida 9 veces por día.
Pepe come una comida **con frecuencia!**
¿Hace usted ejercicio con frecuencia? _____.
¿Hace usted esfuerzo con frecuencia?   _____.

Pepe come una comida **a menudo** (=con frecuencia)
¿Cambia usted la nitroglicerina
  a menudo?   _____.
¿Cambia usted la nitroglicerina
  (NTG) **cada** 6 a 12 meses?   _____.

Translate into Spanish:
Do you take an NTG tablet each/every time
  that you have chest pain? WOW!   _____.
Pepe was in Hawaii.   _____.
Pepe never was in Hawaii.   ____ nunca _____.
Pepe never was ill.   _____.
Pepe had fever.   _____.
Pepe never had fever.   _____.
Pepe never had angina.   _____.
Pepe never had angina with
  the exercise.   _____.
Pepe never walked to the work.   _____.
Pepe never walked one mile.   _____.
Pepe never walked a mile in his life. _____.
Pepe never spit up blood.   _____.
Pepe never spit up blood in his life. _____.

10.5 THE VERB "TO GIVE" (DAR)

VOCABULARY AND STRESS GUIDE

nouns

el resultado	the result
el seguro social	the social security
la recepcionista	the receptionist
el seguro	the insurance
la póliza	the policy
la trabajadora social	the social worker
la información	the information

verbs

dar	to give

preposition

a	to

This verb is conjugated like the verb **ir** (to go). So what? you say. Who remembers how to conjugate the verb "to go"? Well, here's your chance to learn both conjugations then.

	IR	**DAR**
yo	v<u>oy</u>	d<u>oy</u>
él / ella / usted	v<u>a</u>	d_
nosotros	v<u>amos</u>	d____
ellos / ellas / ustedes	v<u>an</u>	d__

I give the pencil to Pepe.

_ ___ __ _____ **a** ___.

Translate into Spanish:

I give the pencil to him.	_____.
I give the pencil to her.	_____.
I give the pencil to you.	_____.
Pepe gives the pencil to me.	_____ mí.
I give the results to him.	_____.
The patient gives his number of social security.	_____.
The patient gives his number of social security to the receptionist.	_____.
The patient gives his number of insurance to the receptionist.	_____.
The patient gives his number of policy to the secretary.	_____.
The patient gives his number of policy to the social worker.	_____.
The patient gives the information to the social worker.	_____.

10.6 INDIRECT OBJECT PRONOUNS

VOCABULARY AND STRESS GUIDE

nouns

el teléfono	the telephone
el at<u>a</u>que al corazón	the heart attack
la vac<u>u</u>na	the vaccine

la receta   the prescription
el permiso   the consent form
la inyección   the injection

adjective
correcto/a   correct

I know, you barely know what indirect object pronouns are in English, so how can I expect you to learn them in Spanish? Briefly, then:

subject	**verb**	**direct object**	**indirect object**
Pepe	gives	the pencil	to Ana.

or:

subject	**verb**	**indirect object pronoun**	**direct object**
Pepe	gives	me	the pencil.

In Spanish, we do almost the same thing except the position of the indirect object pronoun (me, him, her, you, us, them, for you graduates of Mrs. Bostich) is not after the verb as in English (gives me), but **before the verb (to me gives).**

Pepe {to me} gives the pencil.
____   **me**   ____ __ ____
Pepe {to him} gives the pencil.
____   **le**   ___ __ ____
Pepe {to her} gives the pencil.
____   **le**   ___ __ ____
Pepe {to you} gives the pencil.
____   **le**   ___ __ ____

Translate into Spanish:
I to you give the pencil.   _____.
I to him give the pencil.   _____.
I to her give the pencil.   _____.
The patient gives.   _____.
The patient to me gives.   _____.
The patient to me gives the arm.   _____.
The patient to him gives.   _____.
The patient to him gives the bottle.   _____.
The patient to her gives.   _____.

The patient to her gives the
  social security number.   _____.
The patient to you gives.   _____.
The patient to you gives his number
  of telephone.   _____.
I give.   _____.
I to him give.   _____.
I to him give a heart attack.   _____.
I give.   _____.
I to her give.   _____.
I to her give an injection.   _____.
He gives.   _____.
He to me gives.   _____.
He to me gives a heart attack.   _____.
He to him gives a vaccination.   _____.
Give me your arm, please.   **Deme** _____.
Give me the prescription, please.   _____.
Give me the consent form, please.   _____.
Give me the correct consent form,
  please.   _____.

10.7 MY HEAD HURTS

VOCABULARY AND STRESS GUIDE

nouns
la erupción	the rash
el yeso	the cast
el chocolate	the chocolate
la televisión	the television

verbs
molestar	to bother
gustar	to like
mirar	to watch

expressions
¿Le duele?	Does it hurt?
¿Le quema?	Does it burn?
¿Le pica?	Does it itch?

¿Le mo<u>les</u>ta?   Does it bother you?
¿Le <u>gus</u>ta?   Do you like it?

How appropriate that we should finally learn how to say "I've got this blinding headache" in Spanish. Unfortunately, some of you might get one learning how to say it, so I would recommend that you take a couple of aspirin before you go on.

In Spanish, as in English, we frequently (con frecuencia) say:
I have a headache (pain of head).   _____.
But, remember how to say "Does
 your head hurt?" ("Hurts the head?")   _____.
And remember how to say "to me"?   ___.

So to say:
To me hurts the head (that's
 how we say "My head hurts").   _____.
To him hurts the throat.   _____.
To her hurts the breast (same
 as chest).   _____.
To you hurts the finger.   _____.

To ask the question, "Does your finger hurt?" all you need to do is keep the same word order, raise you eyebrows, and put a question mark at the end:

To you hurts the head?   _____?
To him hurts the ankle?   _____?
To her hurts the chest/breast?   _____?
  (Doesn't this ever get confusing, even to native speakers?)
To you stings/burns the urine?   _____?
To you itches the vagina?   _____?
To you itches the eruption (rash)
 of the skin?   _____ la erupción _____?
To you bothers the bandage?   _____ molesta _____?
To you bothers the cast?   _____ el yeso?
To you is pleasing the chocolate?   _____ **gusta** el chocolate?
  (Believe it of not, that's how we say "Do you like chocolate?")
To you is pleasing to walk?   _____?
To you is pleasing to watch
 television?   _____ mirar la televisión?
To you is pleasing to have children? _____?

(If you don't learn how to speak Spanish by the time you finish the <u>Manual</u>, you'll at least speak English as if you did.)

What I suggest now, is that you go back over the corrected answers and repeat them until they are automatic:

¿Le duele la cabeza?
¿Le quema la orina?
¿Le pica el flujo?
¿Le molesta el yeso?
¿Le gusta el chocolate?

10.8 COGNATES

These will come in handy in the Interview.

Nouns: -e becomes -a or -ia; -ion and -sis remain the same; -a and -I remain the same
arteries
angina
nitroglycerine
cholesterol
calories
hyptertension
tension
mode
experience
nicotine
arteriosclerosis

Verbs: add -ar or, more infrequently, -er or -ir
pass
receive
deteriorate

Adjectives: add -a or -o, infrequently -e
ineffective
important

Adverbs: remember -mente
possibly

10.9 KEY CONCEPTS

Yo orino **una vez** por hora.
Yo orino **muchas veces** por hora.
Yo orino en el inodoro **siempre.**
Yo **nunca** orino en el piso.
Cada vez que yo orino, orino en el inodoro.
Deme el brazo, por favor.
¿Le duele la cabeza?
¿Le gusta el chocolate?

Lesson 10

El paciente con angina
(The Patient with Angina)

(translate this out loud)   **(check yourself with this)**

Hello. Good morning.	Hola. Buenos días.
My name is ____	Me llamo____

I am the doctor/
  nurse/medical/
  nursing student.
	Soy el/la doctor/a,
	  enfermero/a, estudiante
	  de medicina/de enfermería.

How are you?	¿Cómo está usted?

Do you know why you
  are here in the hospital today?
	¿Sabe usted porqué usted
	  está aquí en el hospital hoy?

How old are you?	¿Cuántos años tiene usted?
You have pain? Where is the pain?	¿Tiene dolor? ¿Dónde está el dolor?
In the chest?	¿En el pecho?
What is the pain like?	¿Cómo es el dolor?
Is it like a stab?	¿Es cómo una puñalada?
Is it like a constriction?	¿Es cómo una opresión?
Is it like a cramp?	¿Es cómo un calambre?
Is it like a burn?	¿Es cómo una quemadura?

For how long have
  you had this pain?
	¿Hace cuánto tiene
	  el dolor?

Is this the first time
  that you have pain like this?
	¿Es la primera vez
	  que tiene dolor así?

When was the last time
  that you had pain like this?
	¿Cuándo fue la última vez
	  que tuvo dolor así?

Where does the pain go?	¿Adónde va el dolor?
To the neck?	¿Al cuello?
To the left arm?	¿Al brazo izquierdo?
To the jaw?	¿A la mandíbula?
To the teeth?	¿A los dientes?
To the back?	¿A la espalda?

Does the pain get worse with the effort?	¿El dolor empeora con el esfuerzo?
With the exercise?	¿Con el ejercicio?
With the emotions?	¿Con las emociones?
With the cold?	¿Con el frío?
After eating a large meal?	¿Después de comer una comida grande?
Do you have the pain when you are in bed?	¿Tiene usted el dolor cuando está en la cama?
When you are on your feet?	¿Cuando está de pie?
When you are exercising?	¿Cuando hace ejercicio?
Do you take medications?	¿Toma usted medicamentos?
Do you take NTG?	¿Toma usted nitroglicerina?
Does the pain improve with NTG?	¿Mejora el dolor con la NTG?
Does the pain improve if you go to bed?	¿Mejora el dolor si va a la cama?
Do you have difficulty breathing?	¿Tiene dificultad en respirar?
Do you have difficulty breathing at night?	¿Tiene dificultad en respirar a la noche?
Do you have difficulty breathing when you have the chest pain?	¿Tiene dificultad en respirar cuando tiene el dolor de pecho?
I want to ask (make) some questions of your style (mode) of life:	Quiero hacer unas preguntas de su modo de vida:
Do you exercise? How much?	¿Hace usted ejercicio? ¿Cuánto?
With frequency?	¿Con frecuencia?
How much do you weigh?	¿Cuánto pesa?
Do you work?	¿Trabaja usted?
What do you do in your work?	¿Qué hace en su trabajo?
Do you smoke?	¿Fuma usted?
How many packets of cigarettes do you smoke per day?	¿Cuántos paquetes de cigarrillos fuma usted por día?
Do you have hypertension?	¿Tiene hipertensión?
High cholesterol? Diabetes?	¿Colesterol alto? ¿Diabetes?
Is there heart disease in your family?	¿Hay enfermedad del corazón en su familia?

Did your father die of a heart attack?	¿Murió su padre de un ataque al corazón?
How old was your father when he died?	¿Cuántos años tuvo[2] su padre cuando murió?
Do you have much tension in your life? In your family?	¿Tiene usted mucha tensión en su vida? ¿En su familia?

You have angina. Angina is chest pain. When the arteries in the heart have atherosclerosis, the heart does not receive the blood that it needs to work and you get chest pain. This is dangerous because it possibly causes a heart attack if there is no blood that passes through the arteries. You need to have nitroglycerin tablets with you always, and take the tablets when you have chest pain. If one NTG tablet is ineffective, you should take the second tablet. If you have chest pain after 2 or 3 tablets, you should go to the hospital. You should also take NTG before exercise, sexual relations, or emotional experiences. You should change the NTG tablets every 6 to 12 months because they deteriorate. It is important that you not smoke because the nicotine raises your blood pressure and pulse, and that you commence to do exercise to lower your blood pressure and pulse. Also, you should avoid salt (because you have high blood pressure) and fat (because you have high cholesterol) and eat with fewer (use "less") calories to lose weight.

Usted tiene angina. Angina es dolor de pecho. Cuando las arterias en el corazón tienen arteriosclerosis, el corazón no recibe la sangre que necesita para trabajar y usted tiene dolor de pecho. Esto es peligroso porque posiblemente causa un ataque al corazón si no hay sangre que pasa por las arterias. Usted necesita tener tabletas de nitroglicerina con usted siempre, y tomar las tabletas cuando usted tiene dolor de pecho. Si una tableta de nitroglicerina es inefectiva, usted debe tomar la segunda tableta. Si usted tiene dolor de pecho después de dos o tres tabletas, debe ir al hospital. Usted debe tomar la nitroglicerina antes del ejercicio, relaciones sexuales, o experiencias emocionales. Usted debe cambiar las tabletas de nitroglicerina cada 6 a 12 meses porque deterioran.[3] Es importante que usted no fuma[4] porque la nicotina sube la presión y el

---

[2]This verb should really be conjugated in the imperfect tense, which we will not learn. If you keep this in the preterit, you will be understood.

[3]Correctly: **se** deterioran; see reflexive verbs in Lesson 12.

[4]Correctly: Es importante que usted no fum**e**. This is the subjunctive, which we will not study in this book.

pulso, y comenzar a hacer ejercicio para bajar la presión y el pulso. También, usted debe evitar la sal (porque usted tiene presión alta) y grasa (porque usted tiene colesterol alto) y comer con menos calorias para perder peso.

Now, go back to page 4 and look at the "Herpes" paragraph again. How much more can you understand?

Lesson 11. The Future

11.1 THE FUTURE

VOCABULARY AND STRESS GUIDE

nouns

diente   tooth

verbs

evi<u>tar</u>   to avoid
mejo<u>rar</u>   to improve
empeo<u>rar</u>   to worsen
sa<u>car</u>   to take (out)

adjective

peli<u>gro</u>so/a   dangerous

Believe it or not, you already know the future in Spanish, but haven't learned how to use it. Let's review the verb **ir** (to go).

Ana: Yo **voy** al baño 5 veces por día.
Pepe **va** al baño 3 veces por día.
Pepita **va** al baño 4 veces por día.
Nosotros **vamos** al baño 12 veces por día.
Pepe y Pepita **van** al baño 7 veces por día.

Y, usted, ¿cuántas veces **va usted** al baño por día?
Yo _____ al baño _____.
Pepe ___ al baño _____.

Pepita ___ al baño _____.
Usted ___ al baño _____.
Nosotros _____ al baño _____.
Pepe y Pepita ___ al baño _____.

Ahora, yo no voy al baño porque estudio la lección de español. Pero en 10
minutos, cuando la lección termina:

Yo voy a ir al baño.
Yo voy a comer una hamburguesa.
Yo voy a mirar la televisión hasta las 10:30.
Yo voy a dormir a las 11:00.

Ana: ¿Adónde **voy a ir** después de la lección?
Pepe: Usted **va a ir** al baño.
Ana: ¿Qué **voy a comer?**
Pepe: Usted __ __ _____ una hamburguesa.
Ana: ¿Hasta qué hora **voy a mirar** la televisión?
Pepe: Usted __ __ _____ la televisión hasta las 10:30.
Ana: ¿A qué hora **voy a dormir?**
Pepe: Usted _____.

Translate into Spanish:
You are going to sleep.   _____.
Are you going to sleep?   _____.
Are you going to eat tomorrow?   _____.
Are you going to avoid salt?   _____.
Are you going to avoid
  dangerous things?   _____.
Is he going to work with the cast?   _____.
You are going to improve.   _____.
The pain is going to improve.   _____.
The pain is going to get worse.   _____.
The pain in the teeth is going
  to get worse.   _____.
The illness is not going to get
  worse.   _____.
I am going to watch television.   _____.
I am going to take blood.   _____.
I am going to take blood from
  your arm.   _____.

Basically, you can construct the future in Spanish as you do in English by using the verb "to go," the preposition "to," and the verb representing the action you want to place in the future. Huh? Watch:

I work. (Present)	I am going to work. (Future)
I eat. (Present)	I _____ eat. (Future)
I sleep. (Present)	I _____ sleep. (Future)

Yo trabajo. (Presente)	Yo voy a trabajar. (Futuro)
Yo como. (Presente)	Yo ___ _ comer. (Futuro)
Yo duermo. (Presente)	Yo ___ _ dormir. (Futuro)

Note that the first verb "to go" is always conjugated, but the second verb (work, eat, sleep) is not conjugated, remaining in its infinitive form (trabajar, comer, dormir).

yo   **voy**

   él
   ella   **va**
   usted

               + a + infinitivo --> futuro

nosotros   **vamos**

   ellos
   ellas   **van**
   ustedes

11.2 AGO

VOCABULARY AND STRESS GUIDE

nouns
la alergia	the allergy

verb
hace (impersonal)	ago/for

Wasn't **hace** one of those expressions that we went over too quickly? I mean, it never really made any sense to say "hace 2 semanas" back in Lesson Whatever. But being the good students that you are, you filled-in, and pronounced, and corrected, and probably forgot.... Well, here's your chance to learn it.   Unfortunately, it still won't make much sense, even the second time around. In the present tense, **hace** means **for**; in the past tense, it means **ago**.   Remember also, that, instead of saying "My diarrhea began seven days **ago**," we say "My diarrhea began **ago** seven days." Well actually, we don't say that either because we usually say it in Spanish and it doesn't sound anything like that.

Present tense (**hace=for**)

Ana: ¿Pepe, tiene diarrea?
Pepe: Sí, _____?
Ana: ¿Hace cuánto tiene diarrea?
Pepe: **Hace** 2 semanas.
Ana: ¿Pepe, tiene fiebre?
Pepe: Sí, _____?
Ana : ¿Hace cuánto tiene fiebre?
Pepe: _____ 3 días.

Past tense (**hace=ago**)

Ana: ¿Cuándo comenzó la diarrea?
Pepe: **Hace** 2 semanas.
Ana: ¿Cuándo comenzó la fiebre?
Pepe: _____ 3 días.
Ana: _____ (When began the pain?)
Pepe: _____ (Ago 2 days)
Ana: _____ (When began the allergy?)
Pepe: _____ (Ago 10 years)
Ana: _____ (When did you have the operation?)
Pepe: _____ (Ago 5 years)
Ana: _____ (When did you have your last child?)
Pepe: _____ (Ago 11 months)
Ana: _____ (When did you have the accident?)
Pepe: _____ (Ago 1 hour)
Ana: _____ (When did you eat?)
Pepe: _____ (Ago 13 hours)
Ana: _____ (When are you going to eat?)
Pepe: _____ (In 15 minutes)
Ana: _____ (When are you going to go?)
Pepe: _____ (In half an hour)
Ana: _____ (When are you going to commence the treatment?)
Pepe: _____ (In 5 months)

Ana: _____   (When is going to commence the
                                        operation?)

Pepe: _____   (In half an hour)

11.3 MODAL VERBS

VOCABULARY AND STRESS GUIDE

nouns

la ayuda	the help
el bloque (la cuadra)	the city block
el escalón	the step
el resto	the rest
la almohada	the pillow
la bomba	the pump (also the bomb)
la insuficiencia cardíaca	the congestive heart failure

verbs

firmar	to sign
impulsar	to pump
explicar	to explain

modal verbs

poder	to be able to
deber	should
querer	to want to
tener que	to have to
tratar de	to try to

When modal verbs are used **in front of** a second verb, they change the
mood of the second verb (kind of like candlelight). Only the first verb is
conjugated, the second verb takes a free ride as the infinitive. Huh?
Watch:

El paciente **puede** comer.	(The patient can eat.)
El paciente **debe** comer.	(The patient should eat.)
El paciente **quiere** comer.	(The patient wants to eat.)
El paciente **tiene que** comer.	(The patient has to eat.)
El paciente **trata de** comer.	(The patient tries to eat.)

Translate into Spanish:

El paciente **puede** comer.

The patient can speak Spanish.   _____.

The mother of the boy can speak
   English.   _____.

The patient can walk with help.   _____.

The man can walk one block.   _____.

Can you walk one block?   _____.

Can you climb one floor?   _____.

Can you climb one step?   _____.

How many steps can you climb?   _____.

El paciente **debe** comer.

The patient should do exercise.   _____.

The patient should follow a
   strict diet.   _____.

The mother of the child should sign
   the consent form.   _____.

El paciente **quiere** comer.

The patient wants to sleep.   _____.

The boy wants to take off the coat.   _____.

The boy wants to put on the clothes.   _____.

Do you want help?   _____.

El paciente **tiene que** comer.

The boy has to sleep.   _____.

The mother of the boy has to sign
   the consent form.   _____.

First, you have to go to
   the pharmacy.   _____.

First, the blood has to go to
   the heart.   _____.

The heart has to pump the blood to
   the rest of the body.   _____.

The blood has to go to the kidneys.   _____.

Do you have to sleep?   _____.

Do you have to sleep with
   three pillows?   _____.

El paciente **trata de** comer.
The patient tries to sign the
   consent form.   _____.
The patient tries to run.   _____.
The heart is a pump.   _____.
The heart is a pump that tries to
   pump the blood to the kidneys.   _____.
I will try to take away the pain.   _____.
I will try to explain.   _____.
I will try to explain how the heart
   pumps the blood.   _____.

Negatives are easy. Remember that the **no** always goes **in front of** the
verb, which in this case is the first (modal) verb.

El paciente **no puede** caminar.
El paciente **no debe** fumar.
El paciente **no quiere** comer.
El paciente **no tiene que** dormir con dos almohadas.
El paciente **no trata de** mejorar.

Translate into Spanish:
The patient can't climb two steps.   _____.
The mother of the boy can't speak
   English.   _____.
The patient tries to climb two steps
   but he can't.   _____.
When the heart can't pump the blood,
   it is called congestive heart
   failure.   _____.
You should not smoke.   _____.
You should not sign the consent form
   before comprehending [under-
   standing] the operation.   _____.
The boy doesn't want to take off the
   clothes.   _____.
The boy doesn't want to put on the
   robe.   _____.
You don't have to sign the
   consent form.   _____.
Don't you have to go home now?   _____.

To make the future of modal verbs is easy:

Usted **va a poder** comer.
Usted **va a querer** caminar.
Usted **va a tener que** hacer ejercicio.
Usted **va a tratar de** mejorar.

Translate into Spanish:
You will be able to sleep.   _____.
Your mother will want to go.   _____.
You will not have to have
  an operation.   _____.
The patient will try to walk.   _____.

11.4 ONE HAS TO

VOCABULARY AND STRESS GUIDE

verbs
descan<u>sar</u>   to rest

Please, repeat after me and try to avoid thinking:

Para estar sano **hay que** comer bien.
Para estar sano **hay que** hacer ejercicio.
Para estar sano **hay que** dormir 8 horas.
Para estar sano **hay que** descansar.
Para estar sano **hay que** estar contento.
Para estar sano **no hay que** fumar.
Para estar sano **no hay que** comer demasiado.

Ana: Para estar sano, ¿**hay que** comer bien?
Pepe: Sí, para estar sano ____ ____ comer bien.
Ana: Para estar sano, ¿**hay que** hacer ejercicio?
Juan: Sí, _____.
Ana: Para estar sano, ¿**hay que** dormir 8 horas?
Pepe: Sí, _____.
Ana: Para estar sano, ¿**hay que** descansar?
Juan: Sí, _____.
Ana: Para estar sano, ¿**hay que** estar contento?

Pepe: Sí, _____.
Ana: Para estar sano, ¿**hay que** fumar?
Juan: No, para estar sano **no hay que** fumar.
Ana: Para estar sano, ¿**hay que** comer demasiado?
Pepe: No, _____.
(Pero esos Twinkis son tan buenos!!)

Note that this verb, **hay,** is also used in front of a second verb (an infinitive) which is modified in mood. But note that there is no subject here as with the other examples:

subject	**modal verb**	**verb**
El paciente	tiene que	trabajar

Rather, it is impersonal, or general:

modal verb	**verb**
Hay que	trabajar

and means, "one has to work."

11.5 OTHERWISE ...

VOCABULARY AND STRESS GUIDE

verb
regre<u>sar</u>   to return

Pepe: Pepita, su madre tiene que ir a Cleveland.
Pepita: Pero ¿por qué Pepe? Ella está muy cómoda aquí con nosotros.
Pepe: Yo sé, pero yo no estoy muy cómodo con ella.
Pepita: Pero ella no quiere ir. Ella quiere estar aquí por un tiempo más.
Pepe: Usted tiene que decir a su madre que tiene que ir, ¡**si no** yo voy a estar enfermo!
Pepita: ¿Cómo? (This expression is used to mean "WHAT???")
Pepe: Ella tiene que regresar a Cleveland, ¡**si no** yo voy a estar muy nervioso!
Pepita: ¿Cómo?
Pepe: Ella tiene que regresar a Cleveland, ¡__ ____ yo voy a estar muy mal!
Pepita: ¿Cómo?

Pepe: Sí, ¡__ __ yo voy a morir de insuficiencia cardíaca!
Pepita: ¿Cómo?
Pepe: Sí, ¡___ ___ yo voy a ir a vivir con Juan!

11.6 KEY CONCEPTS

Yo voy a sacar sangre del brazo
¿Cuántos bloques puede caminar?
Tiene que firmar el permiso
No debe fumar

Lesson 11

Sacar sangre de la vena y La punción lumbar
(The Venipuncture and The Spinal Tap)

The Venipuncture
(Translate into Spanish)

I am going to explain to you how I am going to take blood from your arm. It is not anything dangerous; I take blood from patients many times a day.

First, one has to be very still. I am going to put this tourniquet on your arm, like this, and I am going to squeeze. Does it hurt? I'm sorry, but it is going to last a little minute, that's all.

Then, I am going to wash your arm with a bit of alcohol. I wait a few seconds. The alcohol has to dry.

Then, I am going to take the needle and pinch your skin. Ready? One, two, three! Ouch! I'm finished. Now I am going to take off the tourniquet. Here's a band-aid for the skin. Thank you.

Sacar sangre de la vena

Le voy a explicar cómo yo le voy a sacar sangre del brazo. No es algo peligroso; yo saco sangre de pacientes muchas veces por día.

Primero, hay que estar muy quieto. Yo voy a poner este torniquete en su brazo, así, y voy a apretar. ¿Le duele? Lo siento, pero va a durdar un minutito, nada más.

Después, voy a limpiar su brazo con un poco de alcohol. Espero unos segundos. El alcohol tiene que secar.[1]

Después yo voy a tomar la aguja y voy a pinchar su piel. ¿Listo? ¡Uno, dos, y tres! ¡AUUU! Ya terminé. Ahora le voy a quitar el torniquete. Aquí tiene una venda para la piel. Gracias.

The Spinal Tap
(Translate into Spanish)

I am going to explain how I am going to do the spinal tap. The most important thing is to be still. You have to be sitting on the bed, with your spine as curved as possible. (Or: you have to be lying down on the bed, on

---

[1]**secarse**, correctly. This is a reflexive verb, which we_will get to in the next lesson.

your right side, with your knees flexed. With your nose, try to touch your chest, and with your knees, try to touch your chest, too.)

First, I am going to clean your back with a brown soap to sterilize the skin. I am going to put a sterile paper on top of your lower back. With my finger, I am going to mark the place where I am going to introduce the needle. Now I am going to inject a bit of Lidocaine in the skin. It is a kind of local anaesthetic so as not to feel the pain of the needle. It is going to sting a little bit. Do you feel the needle? Ouch! I'm sorry. Now do you feel the needle? No? Good. Now I am going to introduce the needle in the space between your vertebrae. Please, don't move. I already have the fluid. Now I am going to take out the needle. I'm finished. You are going to feel a bit of pressure on your back; it is my finger. I am going to wash your back and put a band-aid on your back. You are going to have to lie down for 24 hours, otherwise, you are going to have a terrible headache.

La punción lumbar

Le voy a explicar cómo voy a hacer la punción lumbar. La cosa más importante es estar quieto. Usted tiene que estar sendato en la cama, con la columna lo más curvada posible. (O: usted tiene que estar acostado en la cama, en el lado derecho, con las rodillas dobladas. Con la nariz trate de tocar el pecho y con las rodillas trate de tocar el pecho también.)

Primero voy a limpiar la espalda con un jabón marrón para esterilizar la piel. Voy a poner un papel estéril encima de su cintura. Con mi dedo, voy a marcar el lugar donde voy a introducir la aguja. Ahora voy a inyectar un poco de Lidocaína en la piel. Es un tipo de anestecia local para no sentir el dolor de la aguja. Le va a picar un poquito. ¿Siente la aguja? ¡Ay! Lo siento. ¿Ahora siente la aguja? ¿No? Bien. Ahora voy a introducir la aguja en el espacio entre las vértebras. Por favor, no mueva.² Ya tengo el líquido. Ahora voy a quitar la aguja. Ya terminé. Va a sentir un poco de presión en la espalda; es mi dedo. Yo voy a limpiar la espalda y poner una venda en la espalda. Va a tener que estar acostado 24 horas, ¡si no va a tener un dolor de cabeza terrible!

---

²Correctly, it should be: "no **se** mueva." More on reflexives next lesson.

Now, go back to page 4 and look at the "Herpes" paragraph again. How much more can you understand?

Lesson 12. Reflexive Verbs

12.1 REFLEXIVE VERBS

VOCABULARY AND STRESS GUIDE

nouns

la <u>ca</u>ra   the face

reflexive verbs

la<u>var</u>se   to wash oneself
desper<u>tar</u>se   to wake up
cepi<u>llar</u>se   to brush oneself
du<u>char</u>se   to shower oneself
se<u>car</u>se   to dry oneself
pei<u>nar</u>se   to comb oneself
ves<u>tir</u>se   to dress oneself
lla<u>mar</u>se   to call oneself

Reflexive verbs are just run-of-the-mill verbs whose subject and direct object happen to be the same. Watch:

subject	**verb**	**object**
I	wash	the dog --->is not reflexive because
		subject ≠ object

subject	**verb**	**object**
I	wash	myself ---> is reflexive because
		subject = object

In Spanish, the object (which becomes the reflexive pronoun) is placed, like the indirect object pronoun, **in front of the verb**. Thus:

I   **myself   wash**

Yo   **me   lavo**

In English, we often drop the myself, himself, yourself, etc:

I   **wash   my head**

In Spanish, we always retain the reflexive pronoun (myself, himself, etc.) but drop the possessive pronoun (my, his, yours, etc) because we hate being redundantly possessive.

I myself wash the head.   _____.
I myself wake up.   _____ despierto.
I myself wash the face.   _____ la cara.
I myself brush the teeth.   _____ cepillo _____.
I myself shower.   _____ ducho.
I myself dry the face.   _____ seco _____.
I myself dry the hair.   _____.
I myself comb the hair.   _____ peino _____.
I myself dress.   _____ visto.
I myself call Ana.   _____ (is this beginning
                                         to make sense?)

How yourself call?
  (What's your name?)   _____?
How yourself wash?   _____ lava?
How yourself wash the face?   _____?
How yourself shower?   _____ ducha?
At what time yourself shower?   _____?

Let's make sure you've been doing this correctly:

yo   **me** lavo la cara

él
ella   } **se** lava la cara
usted

Note that you're conjugating the verb as if you were saying:

I	wash
Yo	lav**o**
You	wash
Usted	lav**a**

but adding the reflexive pronoun between the subject and the verb:

Yo	**me**	lav**o**
Usted	**se**	lav**a**

Translate into Spanish:

I wash. _____.

I wash myself. _____.

I wash my face. _____.

I wash. _____.

I wash Pepe's face. _____.

He brushes. _____.

He brushes himself. _____.

He brushes his teeth. _____.

He brushes. _____.

He brushes the patient's hair. _____.

You call. _____.

You call yourself. _____.

You call yourself Juan. _____.

You call. _____.

You call the doctor. _____.

12.2 INVENTING YOUR OWN REFLEXIVE VERBS

VOCABULARY AND STRESS GUIDE

reflexive verbs

bañarse	to bathe oneself
rasurarse	to shave oneself
acostarse	to lie down
ahogarse	to drown, to suffocate

verbs

pen<u>sar</u>   to think

acumu<u>lar</u>   to accumulate

Following is a list of verbs. If the verb can have the same subject and object, then it can be reflexive; if it's improbable, impossible, or plain silly for the subject and object of the verb to be the same (i.e., to eat: I eat myself?) then the verb can't be reflexive. Pick out the reflexive verbs from the following list, write them as reflexive verbs, and make up a sentence. The infinitives of reflexive verbs are formed very simply: take the infinitive of the non-reflexive verb and add -**se** to the end: **lavar + se = lavarse.**

VERBO	¿INFINITIVO REFLEXIVO?	FRASE
<u>lavar</u>	<u>lavarse</u>	<u>Yo me lavo la cara.</u>
<u>tragar</u>	no	<u>Yo trago el agua.</u>
<u>cepillar</u>		
<u>despertar</u>		
<u>duchar</u>		
<u>bañar</u>		
<u>querer</u>		
<u>masticar</u>		
<u>hablar</u>		
<u>secar</u>		
<u>rasurar</u>		
<u>peinar</u>		
<u>pensar</u>		
<u>acostar</u>		
<u>levantar</u>		
<u>fumar</u>[1]		
<u>llamar</u>		
<u>respirar</u>		
<u>ahogar</u>		
<u>correr</u>		
<u>mover</u>		
<u>vestir</u>		
<u>acumular</u>		

---

[1]The reflexive verb **fumarse** means to get stoned.

12.3 SOME COMMON REFLEXIVE VERBS THAT MIGHT NOT SEEM OBVIOUS

The verb "to feel" might not seem like a likely candidate for a reflexive verb; after all, if you make the subject and object of the verb the same, you get "I feel myself," which might not be exactly what you had in mind. But the truth of it is, that in Spanish we do say "I feel myself well" when we want to say "I feel well" and "How do you feel yourself?" when we want to say "How do you feel?" This is no time to be shy. Just go ahead and say it!

How	yourself	feel? (How do you feel?)
_____	_____	**siente** ?
Yourself	feel	sick? (Do you feel sick?)
_____	_____	_____

Translate into Spanish:
Do you feel healthy?   _____.
Do you feel well?   _____.
Do you feel bad?   _____.
Do you feel weak?   _____.
Do you feel strong?   _____.
Do you feel worse?   _____.
Do you feel better?   _____.
Do you feel sad?   _____.
Do you feel happy?   _____.
Do you feel depressed?   _____.
Do you feel like a patient?   _____.
Do you feel like if you suffocate?   _____.
Do you feel like if you suffocate if
  you sleep with one pillow?   _____.

12.3.1 To Hurt Oneself

Finally, a verb in English which is reflexive: to hurt oneself. This verb is reflexive in Spanish, too: **lastimarse.**

Se lastima. (You hurt yourself, present)
Se lastimó. (You hurt yourself, preterit)

Translate into Spanish:
You hurt yourself with the car.   _____.
Did you hurt yourself with the car?   _____.
When did you hurt yourself?   _____.
How did you hurt yourself?   _____.
At what hour did you hurt yourself?   _____.
With what did you hurt yourself?   _____.
Why did you hurt yourself?   _____.

12.3.2 Reflexive Commands

VOCABULARY AND STRESS GUIDE

nouns

la ropa	the clothing
el abrigo	the coat
las joyas	the jewelry
el pantalón	the pants
el lado	the side
la bata	the robe
la ropa interior	the underwear
los anteojos	the eye glasses

verbs

quitarse	to take off
acostarse	to lie down
moverse	to move oneself
ponerse	to put on oneself

adjective

todo	everything

prepositions

arriba	above/up
abajo	below/down

To construct a command in the reflexive is very simple: All you need to do
is to take the verb in its non-reflexive form and make it an order, then add
se to the end and you're in business! Watch:

Command of **lavar** is: ¡**lave!**

_____ + **se** = ¡**lávese**, por favor!

Command of **quitar** (take off) is: _____

_____ + **se** = ¡**quítese**, por favor!

Translate into Spanish:

Take off the hat, please!   _____.

Take off the clothes, please!   _____.

Take off the coat, please!   _____.

Take off the jewelry, please!   _____.

Take off the pants.   _____.

Take off everything, please!   _____.

Take off everything from
  the waist up.   _____ de la cintura arriba.

Take off everything from
  the waist down.   _____.

Command of **acostar** (to lie down) is: ¡**acueste!**

_____ + **se** = ¡**acuéstese**, por favor!

Translate into Spanish:

Lie down on the bed, please!   _____.

Lie down mouth up, please!
  (we don't say "On your back")   _____.

Lie down mouth down, please!
  (we don't say "On your stomach")   _____.

Lie down on your right side.   _____.

Lie down on your left side.   _____.

Lie down here, please!   _____.

Command of **mover** (to move) is: ¡**mueva!**

_____ + **se** = ¡**muévase**, por favor!

Translate into Spanish:

The child moves himself.   _____.

The child moves himself on the bed. _____.

The baby moves himself
  in the uterus.   _____.

Don't move, please!   _____.

Lie down and don't move.   _____.

Command of **poner** is: **¡ponga!**

_____ + **se** = **¡póngase**, por favor!

Translate into Spanish:

Put on the clothes.   _____.

Put on the pants.   _____.

Put on the coat.   _____.

Put on the robe.   _____.

Put on the interior clothes
  (underwear).   _____.

Put on the eye glasses.   _____.

Take off your clothes.   _____.

Put on the robe.   _____.

Lie down on your back.   _____.

Take off your clothes, put on the robe,
  and lie down on your back, please!   _____.

12.4 TO BE MISSING

VOCABULARY AND STRESS GUIDE

nouns

el botón   the button

verbs

mo<u>rir</u>se   to die

cru<u>zar</u>   to cross

fal<u>tar</u>   to be missing, lacking, absent

adjective

nu<u>e</u>vo/a   new

expression

<u>ca</u>si   almost

Ayer, Pepe tuvo un accidente terrible. Casi se muere. Cruzó la calle sin
mirar a la derecha y a la izquierda, y un carro vino muy rápido y lastimó a
Pepe. Perdió un dedo de la mano izquierda, un diente de la boca, y un botón
de la camisa nueva.

Ahora, **falta** un dedo (a finger is missing)

_____ un diente (a tooth is missing)

_____ un botón (a button is missing)

Translate into Spanish:

The tooth is missing.   _____.

The patient is absent.   _____.

The result is missing.   _____.

The analysis is missing.   _____.

The prescription is missing.   _____.

Note that to say, "is missing/is lacking/is absent," we use one word: **falta** (infinitive: **faltar**) and place it in front of the missing/lacking/absent noun. We also use it to denote shortness of breath (SOB):

Pepe has lack of air (SOB)   _____ **falta de aire**.

Translate into Spanish:

Does Pepe have SOB?   _____.

Do you have SOB?   _____.

Do you have SOB when you walk?   _____.

Can you walk 2 blocks without SOB? _____.

How many steps can you climb
  without SOB?   _____.

Do you have SOB at night?   _____.

How long lasts the SOB?   _____.

Do you get up at night?   _____.

Do you have to get up at night?   _____.

Do you have to get up at night to
  open the window?   _____.

Do you run to open the window at
  night because you have SOB?   _____.

12.5 COGNATES

These will come in handy in the following Interview.

Verbs: use your imagination and add -ar

explain

accumulate

replace

Nouns: -cy becomes -cia; -ism remains the same, as does -al and -on; to the others add -a or -o
aneurism
insufficiency
frequency
rest
mineral
potassium
reason

Adjectives: leave it alone if it already ends in -a; words that end in -y change to -io or -ia
extra
circulatory

12.6 KEY CONCEPTS

Yo me llamo
¿Cómo se llama usted?
¿Cómo se siente usted?
¡Quítese la ropa, por favor!
¡Póngase la bata, por favor!
¡Acuéstese boca arriba, por favor!
La falta de aire

Lesson 12

El paciente con falta de aire
(The Patient with Shortness of Breath)

In Spanish, SOB is "la fatiga" which has two meanings: 1) to be tired and 2) to have shortness of breath. Make sure that you're not talking about one thing and the patient about another. Establish this by asking: **¿Tiene falta de aire o está cansado?**

(translate this out loud)

Hello! How do you feel?
Not very well? I'm sorry.
My name is ____.
I am the doctor/nurse/
  medical/nursing student.

What is your name?
How old are you?
Where are you from?
Do you speak a little English?
For how long are you in the
  United States?
Is your family here with you?
I want to say (mean to
  say) not in the hospital
  but in _____ (name of city)?

Are you married?
Do you have children?
Who lives in the house with you?
Do you work?
Where do you work?
Do you like your work?
Do you like ___ (name of city)?

Do you take medications?
Which? Why?

(check yourself with this)

¡Hola! ¿Cómo se siente?
¿No muy bien? Lo siento.
Me llamo ____
Soy el/la doctor/a,
  enfermera, estudiante de
  medicina/enfermería.

¿Cómo se llama?
¿Cuántos años tiene usted?
¿De dónde viene?
¿Habla usted un poco de inglés?
¿Hace cuánto está usted en los
  Estados Unidos?
¿Está su familia aquí con usted?
¿Quiero decir no en el hospital pero
  en _____?

¿Está casado?
¿Tiene usted hijos?
¿Quién vive en la casa con usted?
¿Trabaja usted?
¿Dónde trabaja?
¿Le gusta el trabajo?
¿Le gusta _____?

¿Toma usted medicamentos?
¿Cuáles? ¿Por qué?

What is the name of your doctor?

Do you have difficulty
  breathing?
Do you have SOB?
Is this the first
  time that you have SOB?
When was the last
  time that you had SOB?
Were you in the hospital
  for your SOB before?

Do you have more SOB
  when you walk?
How many blocks can you walk
  without SOB?
How many steps can you climb
  without SOB?
How many floors can you climb
  without SOB?

Do you have SOB when
  you are in bed?
Do you no longer have SOB
  if you get up?

With how many pillows
  do you sleep at night?
What happens if you
  sleep with only one pillow?
Do you feel that you suffocate?
Do you run to open the
  window at night
  because you feel that
  you suffocate?

Do you have a cough?
Do you have sputum?
Of what color is the
  sputum?
How much sputum do you have?

Do you smoke?

¿Cómo se llama su doctor?

¿Tiene dificultad en
  respirar?
¿Tiene falta de aire?
¿Es la primera vez que tiene
  falta de aire?
¿Cuándo fue la última vez que tuvo
  falta de aire?
¿Estuvo usted en el hospital para su
  falta de aire antes?

¿Tiene falta de aire cuando
  camina?
¿Cuántos bloques
  puede caminar sin falta de aire?
¿Cuántos escalones
  puede subir sin falta de aire?
¿Cuántos pisos puede
  subir sin falta de aire?

¿Tiene falta de aire cuando
  está en la cama?
¿No tiene más falta de aire si usted
  se levanta?

¿Con cuántas almohadas
  duerme usted a la noche?
¿Qué pasa si usted duerme
  con una sóla almohada?
¿Se siente que se ahoga?
¿Corre usted a abrir la
  ventana a la noche
  porque se siente que
  se ahoga?

¿Tiene usted tos?
¿Tiene usted esputo?
¿De qué color es el
  esputo?
¿Cuánto esputo tiene?

¿Fuma usted?

How much do you smoke?   ¿Cuánto fuma?
For how long do you smoke?   ¿Hace cuánto fuma usted?

You have congestive heart failure. I will try to explain what this is. The heart pumps blood. First, it receives blood with oxygen from the lungs and it pumps it to the rest of the body. After, it receives the blood without oxygen from the body and it pumps it to the lungs for oxygen. If the pump doesn't work as it should, the blood accumulates itself in the lungs or in the body. Your heart does not work as it should; blood accumulates itself in the lungs and that is the reason why you can't breathe. When the heart doesn't work, the kidneys don't work either. The water accumulates in the body. (That) is the reason why your legs are swollen with extra water. To treat the heart, you need to take these pills. One is called "Digoxin." It will help the heart to work better and to pump the blood from the lungs. This pill is called "Lasix." It will help the kidneys to take off the water that accumulated itself in the legs. You will urinate very much. This last pill is called "Potassium." Frequently, you lose this mineral in the urine. It is important to replace the potassium. Please take all these pills each day, otherwise you will get worse.

Usted tiene insuficiencia cardíaca congestiva. Yo voy a tratar de explicar qué es. El corazón impulsa sangre. Primero, recibe la sangre con oxígeno de los pulmones y la impulsa al resto del cuerpo. Después, recibe la sangre sin oxígeno del cuerpo y la impulsa a los pulmones para el oxígeno. Si la bomba no trabaja como debe, la sangre se acumula en los pulmones o en el cuerpo. Su corazón no trabaja como debe; la sangre se accumula en los pulmones y es la razón porque usted no puede respirar. Cuando el corazón no trabaja, los riñones no trabajan tampoco. El agua se acumula en el cuerpo. Es la razón porque sus piernas están hinchadas con agua extra. Para tratar el corazón usted necesita tomar estas tabletas. Una se llama "Digoxin." Va a ayudar a el corazón a trabajar mejor y a impulsar la sangre de los pulmones. Esta tableta se llama "Lasix." Va a ayudar a los riñones a quitar el agua que se acumuló en las piernas. Usted va a orinar mucho. Esta última tableta se llama "Potasio." Con frecuencia, usted pierde este mineral en la orina. Es importante reemplazar el potasio. Por favor, tome todas estas tabletas cada día, si no usted va a empeorar.

Now, go back to page 4 and look at the "Herpes" paragraph again. Can you understand it all?

EPILOGUE

Well, congratulations. You made it through the <u>Manual</u> and maybe learned a little Spanish ... all without getting *turista* or your traveller's checks stolen ... I suggest that you take a nice hot bath and relax ... you deserve it. Then practice: speak with your patients in Spanish (but only if they're Spanish-speaking or took Spanish in college), speak with any bilingual staff in Spanish and ask them to correct you, listen to the interpreters when you use them, and listen to Spanish radio or television (are you *crazy???*). Above all, remember to **break down, invent (be daring), and pronounce!** It's been fun learning with you, and ¡BUENA SUERTE!

ANSWER KEY

Lesson 1

1.1.5
Los <u>herpes</u> son llagas que parecen como ampollas sin <u>líquido</u>, <u>o</u> una <u>inflamación</u> pequeña. La <u>primera</u> <u>indicación</u> que usted va a <u>notar</u> <u>es</u> una <u>sensación</u> de <u>ardor</u> o de picazón con <u>dolor</u>. Estas llagas pueden <u>aparecer</u> <u>en</u> muchas <u>partes</u>, <u>inclusive</u> los <u>genitales</u> <u>exteriores</u>, los muslos, el <u>perineo</u>, (<u>área</u> <u>entre</u> la <u>vagina</u> y el <u>ano</u>), el ano, o en las nalgas.
Herpes ... liquid, or ... inflamation... first indication ... notice is ... sensation ... ardor or ... pain ... appear in ... parts, including ... genitals exterior ... perineum, (area inter ... vagina ... anus) anus or in ...

1.2
Buenos días.
Buenos días.
¡Buenos días Pepe!
¡Buenos días Juan!
¡Buenos días Ana!
Buenas tardes.
Buenas tardes.
¡Buenas tardes Pepe!
¡Buenas tardes Juan!
Buenas noches.
Buenas noches.
¡Buenas noches Juan!
¡Buenas noches Ana!
El padre se llama Ramón.
El doctor se llama Vásquez.
La doctora se llama Gómez.
La profesora se llama Ana.
El hospital se llama _____
El niño se llama Roberto.
La niña se llama Felisa.
¿Cómo se llama la madre?
¿Cómo se llama el padre?
¿Cómo se llama el niño?
¿Cómo se llama el doctor?
¿Cómo se llama la doctora?
¿Cómo se llama usted?
¿Cómo se llama usted?
Yo me llamo _____
Yo me llamo José. ¿Cómo se llama usted?
El hospital se llama _____
El medicamento se llama Lasix.

1.3
Sí, es el brazo.
Sí, es el codo.
Sí, es el dedo.
No, no es el codo.
No, no es el dedo.
Es el brazo.

Sí, es el dedo.
No, no es el codo.
No, no es el dedo.
Es el brazo.
Es el codo.
Es el dedo.
¿Qué es?
¿Qué es?
¿Qué es?
¿Qué es?
¿Qué es?
¿Qué es?
Es el cuello.
Es el labio.
¿Es el labio o es el ojo? Es el ojo.
¿Qué es?
¿Qué es?
¿Qué es?
No, no es el hombro.
Es el estómago.
¿Es el pecho o es el hombro? Es el hombro.
Es el pecho.
¿Qué es?
¿Qué es?
Sí, es el tobillo.
¿Qué es?
Sí, es la pierna.
No, no es la pierna.
¿Qué es?
¿Es la pierna o es la rodilla? Es la rodilla.
¿Qué es?
¿Qué es?
¿Qué es?
Es la cabeza.
Es la boca.
Es la lengua.
¿Es la lengua o es la cabeza? Es la cabeza.
¿Qué es?
¿Qué es?
¿Qué es?
¿Es la cintura o es la costilla? Es la costilla.
¿Es la costilla o es la espalda? Es la espalda.
¿Qué es?
¿Qué es?
¿Es la mano o es la uña? Es la uña.

1.5

el dedo	la costilla
el hombro	la cintura

el cuello   la boca
el pecho   la lengua
el estómago   la mano

1.6
los labios   las uñas
los tobillos   las costillas
los pies   las manos

los brazos
las bocas
los pechos
las cabezas
los cuellos
las espaldas

1.7
Sí, Ana es la profesora.
No, Ana no es la secretaria.
No, Ana no es la paciente.
No Ana no es la enfermera.
Ana es la profesora.
El presidente de los Estados Unidos es Bush.
¿Quién es el primer ministro de Inglaterra?
Major es el primer ministro de Inglaterra.
¿Quién es el autor de *King Lear*?
Shakespeare es el autor de *King Lear*.
¿Quién es el autor de *El Quijote*?
Cervantes es el autor de *El Quijote*.
No, yo no soy el paciente.
No yo no soy el presidente de los Estados Unidos.
No, yo no soy el autor de *Cien Años de Soledad*.
Yo soy el estudiante.

1.8
Él es el niño.
Él es el paciente.
Ella es la niña.
Ella es la paciente.

1.9
El niño de la madre.
La niña de la madre.
El vaso de agua.
El vaso de vino.
El doctor de pediatría.
El doctor de medicina.
El estudiante de medicina.
El estudiante de medicina de la familia.

El brazo del doctor.
La uña de la enfermera.

1.10
El vaso de agua.
¿Qué es?
color
El sombrero es grande.
¿De qué color es la orina?
¿De qué color es el vino?
El vino es blanco.
¿De qué color es el ojo?
El ojo es negro.
¿De qué color es la sangre?
La sangre es roja.
¿De qué color es la orina?
La orina es amarilla.
¿De qué color es el excremento de la madre?
El excremento de la madre es marrón.
¿De qué color es el esputo del padre?
El esputo del padre es verde.
¿De qué color es el ojo de la niña?
El ojo de la niña es azul.

Lesson 2

2.1
Sí, el lápiz de Pepe es corto.
Sí, el termómetro es corto.
Sí, el lápiz de Juan es largo.
El lápiz de Juan es largo.
No, el lápiz de Pepe no es largo.
El lápiz de Pepe es corto.
El lápiz de Juan es largo.
¿Cómo es el lápiz de Pepe?
¿Cómo es el lápiz de Juan?
¿Cómo es la pierna de Pepe?
¿Cómo es la venda?
¿Cómo es la nariz de Pinoquio? La nariz de Pinoquio es larga.
Sí, el hospital es grande.
Sí, Tejas es grande.
Tejas es grande.
¿Cómo es Delaware? Delaware es pequeño.
¿Cómo es el hospital? El hospital es grande.
La nariz de Thumbellina es pequeña.
¿Cómo es la nariz del Señor Gómez? La nariz del Señor Gómez es grande.
¿Cómo es la nariz de la Señorita Arias? La nariz de la Señorita Arias es mediana.

Sí, Pepe es gordo.
Sí, Laurel es gordo.
Sí, Pepe es bajo.
Sí, Pepe es gordo y bajo.
Sí, Juan es flaco.
Sí, Hardy es flaco.
Sí, Juan es alto.
Sí, Juan es flaco y alto.
No, Pepe no es flaco.
No, Pepe no es alto.
Pepe es gordo y bajo.
Juan es alto y flaco.
Laurel es gordo.
Hardy es flaco.
¿Cómo es Pepe?
¿Cómo es Juan?
¿Cómo es la madre del paciente?
¿Cómo es el padre del niño?

2.2
El brazo es corto.
El cuello es largo.
El dedo es pequeño.
La pierna es corta.
La costilla es larga.
La cintura es pequeña.

2.4
¿Es usted la madre?
¿Es usted el paciente?
¿Es usted la madre del paciente?
¿Es ella la madre?
¿Es él el niño?
¿Es ella la madre del niño?

2.5
La nariz de Ana no es larga.
El hospital no es pequeño.
El presidente Bush no es mejicano.
El sombrero de Juan no es pequeño.

2.6
No, Pepe es gordo pero no es alto.
Sí, Pepe es bajo.
No, Pepe es bajo pero no es flaco.
No, Juan es flaco pero no es bajo.
No, Juan es alto pero no es gordo.
No, Laurel es gordo pero no es alto.

Sí, la nariz de Pinoquio es larga.
No, la nariz de Pinoquio es larga pero no es verde.

2.7
Pepe es más gordo que Juan.
Pepe es más bajo que Juan.
Juan es más flaco que Pepe.
Juan es mas alto que Pepe.
Pepe es más gordo.
Juan es más flaco.
Juan es menos gordo que Pepe.
Juan es menos bajo que Pepe.
Pepe es menos flaco que Juan.
Pepe es menos alto que Juan.
Juan es menos gordo.
Pepe es menos alto.
México es más grande que Nicaragua.
La nariz de Pinoquio es más larga que la nariz de Ana.
El dedo es más corto que la pierna.
grande
más grande que
alto
más alto que
grande
menos grande que
amarillo
menos amarillo que

2.8
No, El Salvador no es grande.
No, Liechtenstein no es grande.
No, Cuba no es grande.
Rusia es un país grande.
Inglaterra es un país pequeño.
¿Cuál es un país hispano? Guatemala es un país hispano.
¿Cuál es un país hispano y grande? Argentina es un país hispano y grande.
¿Cuál es el dedo de Pepe?
¿Cuál es el dedo quebrado?
¿Cuál es el dedo quebrado de Pepe?
¿Cuál es el tobillo quebrado?
¿Cuál es el codo quebrado?
¿Cuál es el brazo de Juan?
¿Cuál es el brazo cortado?
¿Cuál es el brazo cortado de Juan?
¿Cuál es el hombro cortado?
¿Cuál es la uña cortada?
¿Cuál es el pie de Pepe?
¿Cuál es el pie quemado?
¿Cuál es el pie quemado de Pepe?

¿Cuál es la pierna quemada?
¿Cuál es la rodilla quemada?
¿Cuál es el ojo de Juan?
¿Cuál es el ojo hinchado?
¿Cuál es el ojo hinchado de Juan?
¿Cuál es la mano hinchada?
¿Cuál es el tobillo hinchado?
¿Cuál es el dedo infectado?
¿Cuál es el dedo inflamado?

2.9
El dedo corto
El dedo hinchado
El brazo largo
El brazo cortado
El hospital grande
El hospital público
El cuarto privado
La infección roja
La infección seria
La madre seria

2.10
¡No Pepe! No es su venda, ¡es mi venda!
¡No Pepe! No es su libro, ¡es mi libro!
¡No Pepe! No es su lápiz, ¡es mi lápiz!
Sí, es mi venda.
No, Ana, no es su venda, ¡es mi venda!
Sí, es mi libro.
No, Ana, no es su libro, ¡es mi libro!

2.11
¿Quién es el presidente de los Estados Unidos?
¿De quién es la orina?
¿De quién es el niño?
¿De quién es el lápiz blanco?
¿De quién es el café?
¿De quién es el café negro?
¿De quién es el lápiz?

2.12
Yo quiero en cuarto doble, por favor.
Yo quiero el doctor, por favor.
Yo quiero la enfermera, por favor.
¿Quiere usted un cuarto doble?
¿Quiere usted una aspirina?
Sí, gracias, quiero un cuarto privado.
Yo quiero un vaso de agua, por favor.

Yo no quiero el doctor, por favor.

Sí, yo quiero un vaso de agua y una aspirina, por favor.

Sí, gracias, quiero un cuarto privado.

¿Quiere usted el doctor o la enfermera?

¿Qué quiere usted?

¿Quién quiere usted?

Lesson 3

3.1.1

Mi madre se llama Marta.

¿Cómo se llama su padre?

¿Cómo es su padre?

Mi esposo se llama Alex.

¿Cómo es su esposo?

¿Cómo se llama su hijo?

¿Cómo es su hijo?

Mi hermano se llama Roberto.

¿Cómo es su hermano?

Mi hermana se llama Wendy.

¿Cómo es su hermana?

¿Cómo se llama la hija de su hermana?

¿Cómo es la hija de su hermana?

Mi tío se llama Jorge.

¿Cómo es su tío?

Mi tía se llama Inéz.

¿Cómo es su tía?

Mi prima se llama Claudia.

¿Cómo es su prima?

Mi primo se llama Gastón.

¿Cómo es su primo?

Mi abuela se llama Felisa.

¿Cómo es su abuela?

Mi abuelo se llama Antolín.

¿Cómo es su abuelo?

¿Cómo es Andrei?

Mi abuela es vieja.

Mi hijo es joven.

Sí, mi abuela es mayor que mi madre.

Sí, mi abuelo es mayor que mi padre.

¿Es su tío Jorge mayor que su primo Gastón?

Sí, Andrei es menor que Roberto.

Sí, mi madre es menor que mi padre.

¿Es Wendy menor que usted?

3.1.2

La cama de Andrei es pequeña.
La cama de Andrei es cómoda.
Sí, la cama de Andrei es cómoda.
Su cama es incómoda.
Su cama es incómoda.
La cama de Andrei es blanda.
La cama de Andrei es blanda.
Su cama es dura.
Su cama es dura.
Sí, la cama derecha es grande.
La cama derecha es grande.
Sí, la cama izquierda es pequeña.
La cama izquierda es pequeña.

3.1.3

Sí, el tajo en el brazo izquierdo es superficial.
El tajo en el brazo izquierdo es superficial.
Sí, el tajo en el brazo derecho es profundo.
El tajo en el brazo derecho es profundo.
El tajo en el brazo derecho es profundo.
Sí, el dolor en el brazo izquierdo es superficial.
El dolor en el brazo izquierdo es superficial.
¿Cómo es el dolor en el brazo derecho?
¿Cómo es el dolor?
¿Cómo es el dolor?
¿Cómo es el dolor?
¿Cómo es el dolor?
¿Cómo es el dolor?
¿Cómo es el dolor?
¿Cómo es el dolor?
El dolor es progresivamente más severo.
¿Cómo es el dolor?

3.2

La mano de Andrei está mojada.
La mano de Rosa está seca.
La pierna de Roberto está sucia.
La pierna de Marta está limpia.
¿Cómo está la pierna de Marta?
¿Cómo está la frente de Andrei? La frente de Andrei está mojada.
¿Cómo está la camisa de Andrei? La camisa de Andrei está mojada.
¿Cómo está el café?
¿Cómo está el té? El té está caliente.
¿Cómo está el agua? El agua está fría.
¿Cómo está el líquido? El líquido está frío.
¿Cómo está Wendy? Wendy está enferma.

¿Cómo está el esposo de Wendy? El esposo de Wendy no está enfermo, él está sano.
¿Cómo está Claudia? Claudia está embarazada.
No, Wendy no está sana.
Wendy está enferma.
El esposo de Wendy está sano.
Claudia está embarazada.
¿Cómo está Gastón?
¿Cómo está Alex?
¿Cómo está la madre de Alex?
No, Gastón no está resfriado.
No, Gastón no está nervioso.
Gastón está pálido.
Alex está resfriado.
La madre de Alex está nerviosa.
¿Cómo está el paciente?
¿Cómo está Claudia?
¿Cómo está Ana?
No, el paciente no está nervioso.
No, el paciente no está normal.
El paciente está inconciente.
Claudia está embarazada.
Ana está normal.
La temperatura está alta.
¿Cómo está la presión?
La presión está baja.
¿Cómo está el pulso?
El pulso está alto.
Yo estoy resfriada/o.
Yo estoy nerviosa/o.
Yo estoy enferma/o.
¿Cómo está usted?
¿Cómo está usted?
¿Cómo está usted?

3.3

No, el paciente no está en Hawaii.
No, el paciente no está en Acapulco.
No, el paciente no está en Tahiti.
El paciente está en el cuarto.
El cuarto está en el hospital.
El hospital está en San Francisco.
San Francisco está en California.
California está en los Estados Unidos.
¿Dónde está su casa? Mi casa está en _____.
¿Dónde está su madre?
¿Dónde está su padre?
¿Dónde está su familia?
¿Dónde está el dolor? El dolor está en el estómago.
¿Dónde está el dolor? El dolor está en el ombligo.

¿Dónde está el tajo?
¿Dónde está la fractura?
¿Dónde está el dolor?
¿Dónde está el tajo?
¿Dónde está la fractura? La fractura está aquí.
¿Está aquí la fractura?
¿Está aquí el dolor?
¿Está aquí el tajo?
Sí, yo estoy en el hospital.
No, yo no estoy en San Francisco/Sí, yo estoy en San Francisco.
No, yo no estoy en México.
No, yo no estoy en Arizona/Sí, yo estoy en Arizona.
Yo estoy en _____.

3.4.4
El paciente está enfermo.
El paciente es alto.
El paciente está aquí.
El pie es grande.
El pie está sucio.
El pie está en la boca.

3.5
Yo necesito el doctor.
Yo necesito la enfermera.
Yo necesito el cirujano.
¿Necesita usted el doctor?
¿Necesita usted un vaso de agua?
¿Necesita usted el cirujano?
Usted necesita el doctor.
Usted necesita la operación.
Usted necesita la operación del apéndice.
Usted necesita la operación del apéndice inmediatamente.

Lesson 4

4.1
El sombrero está encima de la cabeza.
El paciente está encima de la cama.
El vaso de agua está encima de la mesa.
La cabeza está debajo del sombrero.
La cama está debajo del paciente.
La mesa está debajo del vaso de agua.
La nariz está delante de la cabeza.
La vejiga está delante del útero.
La rodilla está delante de la pierna.
La cabeza está detrás de la nariz.

El útero está detrás de la vejiga.
La pierna está detrás de la rodilla.
La oreja está al lado de la cabeza.
El brazo está al lado del cuerpo.
El riñón está al lado de la aorta.
La oreja derecha está a la derecha de la cabeza.
La oreja izquierda está a la izquierda de la cabeza.
¿Está el dolor encima del ombligo?
¿Está el dolor debajo del útero?
¿Está el dolor encima o debajo del estómago?
¿Está el dolor a la derecha de mi dedo?
¿Está el dolor a la izquierda de mi dedo?
La clínica está detrás del hospital.
El elevador está delante de la clínica.
La farmacia está al lado del hospital.
La sala de emergencia está a la derecha del elevador.

4.2.1   (footnote)
Está seco.
Está caliente.
Está frío.

4.2.3
La botella de Pepe es pequeña.
La botella de Pepe está encima de la mesa.
La tableta es pequeña.
La tableta es blanca.
El vaso de agua está encima de la mesa.
Pepe toma la botella.
No, Pepe no toma la venda.
No, Pepe no toma el vaso de agua.
Pepe toma la botella.
Pepe abre la botella.
No, Pepe no abre la boca.
No, Pepe no abre la mano.
Pepe abre la botella.
Pepe abre la botella y toma la tableta de la botella.
No, Pepe no toma un lápiz de la botella.
No, Pepe no toma una venda de la botella.
Pepe toma la tableta de la botella.
Pepe pone la tableta en la boca.
No, Pepe no pone la tableta en la botella.
No, Pepe no pone la tableta debajo de la mesa.
Pepe pone la tableta en la boca.
Pepe mastica la tableta.
No, Pepe no mastica la botella.
No, Pepe no mastica la mesa.
Pepe mastica la tableta.
Pepe toma el vaso de agua.

Pepe bebe el agua.
No, Pepe no bebe Coca-Cola.
No, Pepe no bebe vino.
Pepe bebe el agua.
Pepe traga la tableta y el agua.
No, Pepe no traga las vitaminas.
No, Pepe no traga la tableta de hierro.
Pepe traga la tableta y el agua.
Pepe pone el vaso de agua encima de la mesa.
Pepe cierra la botella.
No, Pepe no cierra la boca.
No, Pepe no cierra el ojo.
Pepe cierra la botella.
Pepe pone la botella encima de la mesa.

4.2.5

masticar	yo mastico	él mastica
tragar	yo trago	él traga
cerrar	yo cierro	él cierra
hablar	yo hablo	él habla
toser	yo toso	él tose
poner	yo pongo	él pone
vivir	yo vivo	él vive

Yo hablo español.
Usted habla español.
¿Habla usted inglés?
¿Habla usted inglés o español?
¿Toma usted vitaminas?
¿Toma usted hierro?
¿Qué antibióticos toma usted?
Yo tomo el elevador.
¿Fuma usted?
¿Pone usted la tableta debajo de la lengua?
¿Vive usted en Los Angeles?
¿Vive usted con su madre?
¿Vive usted con su esposo/a?
¿Vive usted sin su familia?
¿Vive usted sin su hijo?
¿Vive su hijo con su hija en El Salvador?
¿Toma usted café?
¿Toma usted café con o sin leche?
¿Toma usted café con azúcar?
¿Toma usted té sin azúcar?

Lesson 5

5.1
Ana va a la clínica de la obstetra.
Pepe va a la clínica de la obstetra.
No, Ana no va a la oficina.
No, Ana no va a su casa.
Ana va a la clínica de la obstetra.
No, Ana no va a la clínica con Juan.
Ana va a la clínica con Pepe.
Pepe va a la clínica de la obstetra.
Juan va al hospital.
El Señor Gómez va al hospital.
No, el dolor no va al brazo derecho.
No, el dolor no va a la pierna derecha.
No, el dolor no va a la nariz.
¿Adónde va el dolor?
¿Adónde va el dolor?
¿Adónde va el dolor?
Yo voy a mi casa.
Yo voy al hospital.

5.2
¿Dónde está el dolor?
¿Adónde va el dolor?
¿Dónde está el calor?
¿Adónde va el calor?
¿Dónde está la sensación?
¿Adónde va la sensación?
¿Dónde está la sensación en su pecho?
¿Adónde va la sensación en su pecho?

5.3
Pepe toma aspirina porque está enfermo.
Pepe toma aspirina porque está enfermo.
No, Pepe no toma aspirina porque está bien.
No, Pepe no toma aspirina porque está sano.
Pepe toma aspirina porque está enfermo.
Pepe toma medicamentos porque está enfermo.
¿Por qué toma Pepe calmantes?
¿Por qué toma Pepe antibióticos? Pepe toma antibióticos porque está mal.
¿Por qué está Pepe sentado? Pepe está sentado porque está cansado.
¿Por qué está Ana de pie? Ana está de pie porque no está cansada.
¿Por qué va Juan a la cama? Juan va a la cama porque está cansado.
¿Por qué está Juan en la cama? Juan está en la cama porque está dormido.
¿Por qué no está Ana en la cama? Ana no está en la cama porque no está dormida.
¿Por qué está Pepe triste? Pepe está triste porque está enfermo.
¿Por qué está Ana contenta? Ana está contenta porque no está enferma.

¿Por qué está Pepe preocupado? Pepe está preocupado porque está enfermo.
¿Por qué está Juan cansado? Juan está cansado porque está deprimido.
¿Por qué está Ana contenta? Ana está contenta porque está fuerte.
¿Por qué está Pepe deprimido? Pepe está deprimido porque está débil.
¿Por qué está usted deprimido/a?
¿Por qué está su madre cansada?
¿Por qué no está su madre más fuerte?
¿Por qué toma usted medicamentos?
¿Por qué no toma usted el último medicamento?
¿Por qué no va usted al baño?
¿Por qué no va usted al último baño con la enfermera?

5.4
¿Tiene usted dolor de estómago?
¿Tiene usted diarrea?
¿Tiene usted náusea?
¿Tiene usted vómitos?
¿Tiene usted anemia?
¿Tiene usted tos?
¿Tiene usted fiebre?
¿Tiene usted náusea con el dolor?
¿Tiene usted vómito rosado? Sí, yo tengo vómito rosado.
¿Tiene usted fiebre con el dolor? Sí, yo tengo fiebre con el dolor.
¿Tiene usted dolor con la tos? Sí, yo tengo dolor con la tos.
¿Tiene usted orina oscura? Sí, yo tengo orina oscura.
¿Tiene usted anemia?
¿Tiene usted gastritis?
¿Tiene usted bronquitis?
¿Tiene usted apendicitis?
¿Tiene usted hepatitis?
¿Tiene usted diabetes?
¿Tiene usted hipertensión?
¿Tiene su padre tuberculosis?
¿Tiene usted pancreatitis?
¿Tiene su madre pancreatitis?
¿Tiene usted artritis?
¿Tiene su abuela artritis?
¿Tiene usted celulitis?

5.5
Hace 3 años.
Hace 3 años.
Hace 3 años.
Hace 2 años.
Hace 2 semanas.
¿Hace cuánto tiene vómitos?
¿Hace cuánto tiene fiebre?
¿Tiene náusea?
¿Hace cuánto tiene náusea?

¿Tiene calambres?

¿Hace cuánto tiene calambres?

¿Tiene orina oscura?

Sí, tengo orina oscura.

¿Hace cuánto tiene orina oscura?

¿Hace cuánto tiene fiebre?

¿Hace cuánto tiene vómitos?

¿Tiene náusea? ¿Hace cuánto tiene náusea?

¿Tiene calambres? ¿Hace cuánto tiene calambres?

¿Tiene dolor en el pecho? ¿Hace cuánto tiene dolor en el pecho?

¿Toma antibióticos? ¿Hace cuánto toma antibióticos?

¿Toma drogas? ¿Hace cuánto toma drogas?

¿Fuma usted? ¿Hace cuánto fuma usted?

¿Vive usted en Santa Fe? ¿Hace cuánto vive en Santa Fe?

¿Va usted a la escuela? ¿Hace cuánto va a la escuela?

5.6

El bebé toma leche 5 veces por día.

No, el bebé no toma leche 4 veces por día.

No, el bebé no toma leche 3 veces por día.

El bebé toma leche 5 veces por día.

El bebé toma agua 2 veces por día.

El bebé toma leche de pecho 3 veces por día.

¿Cuántas veces toma Formula por día?

El bebé toma Formula 3 veces por día.

¿Cuántas veces toma la mamadera por día?

El bebé toma la mamadera 3 veces por día.

¿Cuántas veces elimina por día?

El bebé elimina 4 veces por día.

¿Cuántas veces orina por día?

El bebé orina 5 veces por día.

¿Cuántas veces toma vitaminas por día?

¿Cuántas veces da el pecho la mamá?

La mamá da el pecho 3 veces por día.

¿Cuántas veces orina usted por noche?

¿Cuántas veces elimina usted por día?

¿Cuántas veces mueve usted el vientre?

¿Cuántas veces mueve usted el brazo?

¿Cuántas veces da el pecho?

¿Cuántas veces toma usted tabletas?

¿Cuántas veces tiene usted contracciones?

¿Cuántas veces tiene usted contracciones regulares?

¿Cada 5 minutos?

¿Cuántas veces bebe el bebé leche de pecho?

¿Cada 2 horas?

¿Cuántas veces bebe usted bebidas alcohólicas?

¿Muchas veces?

¿Una vez?

Lesson 6

6.1
Sí, Pepe tiene una nariz.
Sí, Pepe tiene dos brazos.
No, Juan no tiene tres piernas.
No, Juan no tiene cuatro manos.
Sí, Pepe tiene cinco dedos en la mano derecha.
No, Juan no tiene seis dedos en la mano izquierda.
No, Pepe no tiene siete cabezas.
No, Juan no tiene ocho tobillos.
No, Pepe no tiene nueve codos.
Sí, Juan tiene diez dedos.
trece
catorce
quince
Diez más uno es igual a once.
Diez más dos es igual a doce.
Diez más tres es igual a trece.
Diez más cuatro es igual a catorce.
Diez más cinco es igual a quince.
diez y ocho
diez y nueve
Diez más seis es igual a diez y seis.
Diez más siete es igual a diez y siete.
Diez más ocho es igual a diez y ocho.
Diez más nueve es igual a diez y nueve.
veinte y dos
veinte y tres
veinte y cinco
veinte y ocho
treinta y nueve
cuarenta y cuatro
cincuenta y siete
sesenta y seis
setenta y cinco
ochenta y dos
noventa y nueve
ciento y siete
tres cientos
cuatro cientos
seis cientos
siete cientos
ocho cientos
novecientos
tres mil cuatro cientos sesenta y siete
cinco mil novecientos ochenta y dos

6.2
¿Qué hora es?
¿Qué es?
they are the 4
they are the 7
son las tres
son las cuatro
son las cinco
son las seis
son las siete
son las ocho
son las nueve
son las diez
son las once
son las doce
son las tres y diez
son las cuatro y quince
son las cinco y treinta
son las diez y treinta y cinco
son las siete menos veinte
son las ocho menos quince (cuarto)
son las nueve menos diez
son las once menos cinco

6.3
¿Qué hora?
La clínica abre.
La clínica cierra.
¿A qué hora abre la clínica?
¿A qué hora cierra la clínica?
¿A qué hora abre la farmacia?
¿A qué hora va el paciente al hospital?
¿A qué hora va su madre a la cita?
¿A qué hora va su madre a la cita con la ginecóloga?
¿A qué hora comienza el dolor?
¿A qué hora comienza el ardor?
¿A qué hora termina el ardor?
¿A qué hora termina el dolor en la cintura?
¿A qué hora comienza el dolor en las nalgas?
¿A qué hora termina la sensación en los muslos?

6.4
son las dos
a las dos
a las cuatro
a las cinco y cinco
a las siete menos cuarto
La cita comienza a las ocho y cinco.

El dolor en los muslos comienza a las ocho y cinco de la mañana.
La cita con la ginecóloga termina a las cinco de la tarde.
El ardor en el perineo comienza a las tres de la tarde.
El ardor en el perineo comienza a las once de la noche.

6.5
¿Cuándo tiene vómitos?
Yo tengo vómitos a la mañana.
¿Cuándo tiene náusea?
Yo tengo náusea a la tarde.
¿Cuándo tiene dolor en la cintura?
Yo tengo dolor en la cintura a la noche.
¿Cuándo tiene la sensación en los muslos?
Yo tengo la sensación en los muslos a la mañana.
¿Cuándo comienza la cita con el doctor?
¿Cuándo termina el examen?
El examen termina en quince minutos.
¿Cuándo comienza el tratamiento?
El tratamiento comienza en un mes.

6.6
Usted pone el condón en el pene antes de tener relaciones sexuales.
Pero usted tiene relaciones sexuales después de poner la jalea o la espuma en la vagina.

6.6.1
antes de cerrar
antes de masticar
antes de tragar
antes de comenzar
antes de respirar
antes de orinar
antes de eliminar
antes de trabajar
antes de limpiar
después de poner
después de beber
después de mover
después de toser
después de comer
después de comprender
después de aprender
antes de abrir
después de venir
antes de ir
después de vivir
antes de sufrir
Antes de comenzar el tratamiento
Antes de comprender cómo tomar el medicamento
Después de tragar el veneno

Después de limpiar las partes privadas
Después de vivir en El Salvador con su madre

Lesson 7

7.1
la abnormalidad
la capacidad
la debilidad
la deformidad
la dificultad
la posibilidad
la regularidad
la enfermedad
Pepe is sick
Rosa is sick
El Señor López está enfermo
La Señora López está enferma
The sick man is in the hospital
The sick woman is in the hospital
El enfermo tiene diarrea
La enferma tiene diarrea
messenger
lechero means milkman
frutero means fruit man
enfermero means nurse, m. (one who deals with sick people)
enfermera means nurse, f. (one who deals with sick people)
the illness
sick, m
sick, f
the sick man
the sick woman
the nurse, m
the nurse, f

7.2
Sí, la mano quema.
¿Quema el codo?
¿Quema el ojo? Sí, el ojo quema.
¿Quema la garganta? Sí, la garganta quema.
¿Quema el estómago después de comer?
¿Quema el estómago antes de comer?
¿Quema el estómago cuando usted come?
¿Quema cuando usted come?
¿Quema cuando usted orina?
¿Quema cuando usted elimina?

¿Quema cuando usted traga?
Sí, la pierna pica.
¿Pica la cabeza?
¿Pica la piel? Sí, la piel pica.
¿Pica el pie? Sí, el pie pica.
¿Pica cuando usted orina?
¿Pica cuando usted elimina?
¿Pica cuando usted traga?
Sí, el ojo duele.
¿Duele el pie?
¿Duele la espalda? Sí, la espalda duele.
¿Duele la llaga? Sí, la llaga duele.
¿Duele la llaga en la piel?
¿Duele la garganta?
¿Duele la garganta cuando traga?
¿Duele cuando usted orina?
¿Duele cuando usted respira?
¿Duele cuando usted come?
Sí, el pie huele mal.
¿Huele mal la axila?
¿Huele mal la orina? Sí, la orina huele mal.
La orina huele mal.
¿Cómo huele el excremento? El excremento huele mal.
¿Cómo huele el flujo?
¿Cómo huele el flujo de la vagina?
¿Cómo huele el flujo de la llaga?
¿Cómo huele el flujo de la herida?
¿Cómo huele el pus?
¿Cómo huele el pus de la herida?
it burns
it   itches/stings
it hurts
it smells
does it burn?
does it itch/sting?
does it hurt?
does it smell?
¿quema?
¿pica?
¿duele?
¿huele?
¿Quema cuando usted orina?
¿Pica cuando usted traga?
¿Duele cuando usted tiene relaciones sexuales?
¿Huele cuando usted mueve el vientre?

7.3
Yo sé hablar en inglés.
Yo sé abrir la puerta.

Yo sé cerrar la puerta.
Yo no sé hablar en español.
Yo no sé cerrar la puerta.
¿Sabe usted hablar en inglés?
¿Sabe usted tomar el medicamento?
¿Sabe usted cuándo tomar el medicamento?
¿Sabe usted cuándo comienza el dolor?
¿Sabe usted qué comienza el dolor?
¿Sabe usted cuándo comienza el picazón?
¿Sabe usted cuándo comienza el picazón de los genitales?
¿Sabe usted qué comienza la molestia?
¿Sabe usted qué comienza la molestia de las partes privadas?
¿Sabe usted qué comienza el picazón del ano?
¿Sabe usted el nombre de su doctor?
¿Sabe usted el nombre se su calle?
¿Sabe usted el número de su calle?
¿Sabe usted el número de su seguro médico?

7.4

Usted habla más despacio.
¡Hable más despacio, por favor!
Usted orina en el inodoro.
¡Orine en el inodoro, por favor!
Usted respira profundo.
¡Respire profundo, por favor!
Usted habla rápido.
¡No hable rápido, por favor!
¡No orine aquí, por favor!
¡Tome dos tabletas cada día, por favor!
Usted come más despacio.
¡Coma más despacio, por favor!
¡Tome leche, por favor!
¡No coma antes de la operación, por favor!
Usted vive en California.
¡Viva en California, por favor!
¡Viva con su madre, por favor!
¡No abra la boca, por favor!
¡No sufra, por favor!
Yo tengo.
¡Tenga la botella, por favor!
¡Tenga el niño, por favor!
¡No tenga relaciones sexuales antes del tratamiento, por favor!
Yo pongo.
¡Ponga la tableta debajo de la lengua, por favor!
¡No ponga la crema encima del labio antes de comer, por favor!
¡No ponga la crema encima de la piel del bebé, por favor!

7.5

aprender	yo aprendo	ud. aprende	¡aprenda!
cerrar	yo cierro	ud. cierra	¡cierre!
comenzar	yo comienzo	ud. comienza	¡comienze!
eliminar	yo elimino	ud. elimina	¡elimine!
comprender	yo comprendo	ud. comprende	¡comprenda!
estar	yo estoy	ud. está	¡esté!
hablar	yo hablo	ud. habla	¡hable!
masticar	yo mastico	ud. mastica	¡mastique!
orinar	yo orino	ud. orina	¡orine!
querer	yo quiero	ud. quiere	¡quiera!
respirar	yo respiro	ud. respira	¡respire!
sufrir	yo sufro	ud. sufre	¡sufra!
terminar	yo termino	ud. termina	¡termine!
toser	yo toso	ud. tose	¡tosa!
trabajar	yo trabajo	ud. trabaja	¡trabaje!
tragar	yo trago	ud. traga	¡trague!
vivir	yo vivo	ud. vive	¡viva!
vomitar	yo vomito	ud. vomita	¡vomite!

Lesson 8

8.1

las heridas inflamadas
las puntadas limpias
las tareas simples
las tareas fáciles
las instrucciones buenas
las cicatrices largas
las familias difíciles
las doctoras ocupadas
las mujeres buenas
las mujeres ricas
las úlceras infectadas
las iglesias grandes
los huesos infectados
los tajos profundos
los problemas serios
los planes temporarios
los pesos bajos
los trabajos permanentes
los documentos largos
los baños ocupados
los hombres pobres
los países pobres

8.2

infinitive	yo	usted	nosotros	ustedes	por favor
to breathe	respiro	respira	respiramos	respiran	¡respire!
curar	curo	cura	curamos	curan	¡cure!
sanar	sano	sana	sanamos	sanan	¡sane!
levantar	levanto	levanta	levantamos	levantan	¡levante!
to concentrate	concentro	concentra	concentramos	concentran	¡concentre!
to urinate	orino	orina	orinamos	orinan	¡orine!
to vomit	vomito	vomita	vomitamos	vomitan	¡vomite!
to smoke	fumo	fuma	fumamos	fuman	¡fume!
to eat	como	coma	comemos	comen	¡coma!
aprender	aprendo	aprende	aprendemos	aprenden	¡aprenda!
to suffer	padezco	padece	padecemos	padecen	¡padezca!
to live	vivo	vive	vivimos	viven	¡viva!
perder	pierdo	pierde	perdemos	pierden	¡pierda!
dormir	duermo	duerme	dormimos	duermen	¡duerma!
morir	muero	muere	morimos	mueren	¡muera!
sentir	siento	siente	sentimos	sienten	¡sienta!
seguir	sigo	sigue	seguimos	siguen	¡siga!

8.2 (footnote)

¿Padece usted de los riñones?
¿Padece usted del higado?
¿Padece usted de cancer?
¿Padece usted de hipertensión?

8.2

¡Siga las instrucciones, por favor!
¡Siga las instrucciones del doctor, por favor!
¡Siga la línea negra a la farmacia, por favor!
¿Quiere usted trabajo?
¿Quiere usted sus documentos?
¿Quiere usted dinero?
¿Quiere usted más dinero?
¿Quiere usted fumar?
¿Quiere usted levantar la pierna?
¿Quiere usted comer?
¿Quiere usted dormir?
¿Quiere usted morir?
¿Qué quiere usted?
¿Qué piensa usted?
¿Qué pierde usted?

8.3

If el dedo means the finger, then un dedo means a finger, and if la cabeza means the head, then una
  cabeza means a head.
No, no hay dos presidentes.
No, no hay tres presidentes.
Hay un presidente.

¿Cuántos senadores hay en Oklahoma?
¿Cuántos estados hay en los Estados Unidos?
¿Cuántas cabezas hay en el cuerpo?
¿Cuántas semanas hay en un año?
No, no hay un estómago encima de la cabeza.
No, no hay un riñón encima de la cabeza.
Hay pelo encima de la cabeza.
Hay un cuello encima de la cabeza.
¿Qué hay a la derecha de la cabeza?
¿Qué hay a la izquierda de la cabeza?
¿Qué hay en la cabeza?
Sí, hay pelo encima de la cabeza.
¿Hay cáncer en su familia?
¿Hay artritis en su familia?
¿Hay alcoholismo en su familia?
¿Hay suicidas en su familia?
¿Hay tuberculosis en su familia?
¿Hay enfermedad del corazón en su familia?

8.4
Porque usted es muy gordo.
Sí, usted necesita un dieta estricta.
Sí, usted necesita comer menos.
Sí, usted necesita perder peso.
Sí, usted necesita hacer ejercicio.
Debe comer menos sal.
Debe comer sin sal.
Debe comer menos grasa.
Debe hacer más.
Debe hacer más ejercicio.
Debe seguir una dieta sin sal.
No debe comer más que un huevo una vez por semana.
No debe fumar.
No debe caminar después de la operación.

8.5
Dra: ¿Es cómo una opresión?
Dra: ¿Es cómo un calambre?
Pepe: No, no es cómo un calambre.
Dra: ¿Es cómo una quemadura?
Pepe: Sí, es cómo una quemadura.
Dra: ¡Basta de comer esos Twinkis!

8.6
Dra: Así. (and she rotates the foot to indicate how to do it)
Dra: Así.
Dra: Así.
Dra: Así.
Dra: Así.

Dra: Así.
Dra: Así.

8.7
Yo como desde las 12 hasta la 1.
El desayuno comienza a las 7 de la mañana.
El desayuno termina a las 7:30 de la mañana.
El almuerzo comienza a las 12.
El almuerzo termina a la 1.
El almuerzo dura una hora.
No, el desayuno no dura 12 horas.
No el desayuno no dura 11 horas.
El desayuno dura 30 minutos.
El almuerzo dura 1 hora.
¿Cuánto tiempo dura la cena?
¿Cuánto tiempo dura el examen?
¿Cuánto tiempo dura el examen pélvico?
¿Cuánto tiempo dura el ataque?
¿Cuánto tiempo dura el ataque de nervios?
¿Cuánto tiempo dura la depresión?
¿Cuánto tiempo dura la ansiedad?
¿Cuánto tiempo dura la desesperación?
¿Cuánto tiempo dura la tristeza?

8.8
¡Pepe duerme demasiado!
¡Pepe fuma demasiado!
Juan no duerme suficiente.
Juan no hace ejercicio suficiente.
Juan trabaja demasiado.
La presión es demasiado baja.
El pulso es demasiado alto.
El pulso es demasiado bajo.

8.9
¿Está el dolor en la cabeza?
¿Está el ardor en el ojo?
¿Está la muerte fuera de la familia?
¿Está la suicida en la familia?
¿Están los hombres empleados en la casa?
¿Su hermana casada vive en la casa con usted?

8.10
Esta tableta es para el dolor.
Esta tableta es para la diarrea.
Estas tabletas son para el dolor.
Estas tabletas son para la fiebre.
¿Para qué son estas tabletas?
Estas tabletas son para quitar el dolor.

Estas tabletas son para quitar la diarrea.
Estas tabletas son para quitar la depresión.
Estas tabletas son para quitar el agua.
Estas tabletas son para bajar la presión.
Estas tabletas son para bajar el colesterol.
Estas tabletas son para subir el hierro en la sangre.
Estas tabletas son para subir el potasio.
¿Está usted?
¿Está usted preocupada?
¿Está usted preocupada por el dinero?
¿Está usted preocupada por la salud?
¿Está usted preocupada por la salud de su esposo?
¿Está usted preocupada por el entretenimiento?

8.11
La dificultad
dificultad
Dificultad en tomar
Dificultad en tomar decisiones
Dificultad en tomar decisiones difíciles
Dificultad en trabajar
Dificultad en pensar
Dificultad en dormir
Dificultad en concentrar

Lesson 9

9.1
Dra: ¿Fue usted a la casa de su tío ayer?
Dra: ¿Abrió el garage ayer?
Dra: ¿Qué abrió usted ayer?
Dra: ¿Habló con Marcos ayer?
Dra: ¿Con quién habló usted ayer?
Dra: ¿Tomó la venda ayer?
Dra: ¿Qué tomó usted ayer?
Pepe: No, Pepita no gritó ayer.
Dra: ¿Gritó Juan ayer?
Dra: ¿Quién gritó ayer?
Dra: Y después, ¿usted respiró?
Y después, ¿usted cerró la puerta?
Y después, ¿usted llamó a Pepita?
Y después, ¿usted sintió un dolor?
Y después, ¿usted sintió un dolor en la espalda?
Sí, yo fumé ayer.
Sí, yo respiré ayer.
Sí, yo hablé ayer.
Sí, yo vomité ayer.

Sí, yo estornudé ayer.
Sí, yo causé un accidente ayer.
Sí, yo bebí ayer.
Sí, yo tosí ayer.
Sí, yo aprendí ayer.
Sí, yo perdí ayer.
Sí, yo viví ayer.
Sí, yo sufrí ayer.
Sí, yo seguí ayer.
Sí, yo dormí ayer.
Sí, yo salí ayer.

9.2
Hoy es martes.
Ayer fue lunes.
Hoy es miércoles.
Ayer fue martes.
Hoy es jueves.
Ayer fue miércoles.
Hoy es viernes.
Ayer fue jueves.
Hoy es sábado.
Ayer fue viernes.
Hoy es domingo.
Ayer fue sábado.
Hoy es lunes.
Ayer fue domingo.
Ahora, Pepe va a la ventana.
Ayer, Pepe fue a la ventana.
Ahora, Pepe va a la casa de Juan.
Ayer, Pepe fue a la casa de Juan.

9.3
Pepe: Sí, Pepita estuvo en la escuela ayer.
Pepe: Sí, Pepita estuvo en la clínica ayer.
Dra: ¿Estuvo usted en Hawaii ayer?
Dra: ¿Estuvo usted en Tahiti el mes pasado?
¿Estuvo usted en el hospital el año pasado?
¿Estuvo usted en la cárcel el mes pasado?
¿Estuvo usted en un país con aire contaminado?
¿Estuvo usted en un cuarto con humo?

9.4
Pepe: Sí, Pepita tuvo escalofríos ayer.
Pepe: Sí, yo tuve un accidente.
Dra: ¿Tuvo usted un resfrío la semana pasada?
Dra: ¿Tuvo usted emociones fuertes ayer?

9.5

Dra: ¿Tiene usted dolor de estómago?
Dra: Por favor, señora, ¿qué dice el niño?
Dra: ¿Tiene usted diarrea?
Madre: El niño dice que tiene diarrea.
El niño dice que tiene náusea.
El niño dice que tiene asma.
El niño dice que tiene un gato en la casa.
El niño dice que tiene un perro en la casa.
El niño dice que tiene muchos animales en la casa.
El niño dice que hace ejercicio.
El niño dice que no hace ejercicio.

9.6

La farmacia está en el primer piso.
La cafetería está en el segundo piso.
El departamento de cirugía está en el tercer piso.
La sala de cuidado intensivo está en el cuarto piso.
El departamento de cardiología está en el quinto piso.
El departamento de pediatría está en el sexto piso.
El departamento de psiquiatría está en el último piso.

9.7

¿Tiene?
¿Hace cuánto tiene?
primer
vez
que
¿Tuvo usted?
cuando
fue
último

¿Tiene usted diarrea?
¿Hace cuánto tiene usted diarrea?
¿Es la primera vez que tiene diarrea?
¿Cuándo fue la última vez que tuvo diarrea?
¿Respira usted con silbidos?
¿Hace cuánto respira usted con silbidos?
¿Es la primera vez que respira con silbidos?
¿Cuándo fue la última vez que respiró con silbidos?
¿Toma usted medicamentos?
¿Hace cuánto toma usted medicamentos?
¿Es la primera vez que toma medicamentos?
¿Cuándo fue la última vez que tomó medicamentos?
¿Está usted embarazada?
¿Hace cuánto está usted embarazada?
¿Es la primera vez que usted está embarazada?
¿Cuándo fue la última vez que estuvo embarazada?

Lesson 10

10.1
Se fuma en el cuarto privado.
No se fuma en el cuarto privado.
Se habla español en México.
Se introduce un catéter en el brazo.
No se fuma en la sala de emergencia.
No se fuma en la sala de partos.
No se fuma en la sala de cuidado intensivo.
No se corre aquí.
¿Cómo se dice "kidneys" en español?
¿Cómo se dice "liver" en español?
¿Cómo se escribe su nombre?
¿Cómo se escribe su apellido?

10.2
Juan: No sé si Al Pacino está en Nueva York ahora.
Juan: No sé si Dustin Hoffman está en San Francisco ahora.
Dra: No sé si Pepita está embarazada.
Dra: No sé si el análisis es positivo.
Dra: No sé si el análisis es negativo.

10.3
¿Tiene usted?
¿Tiene usted diarrea?
¿Tiene usted indigestion?
¿Tiene usted escalofríos?
¿Tiene usted alergia a la aspirina?
¿Tiene usted alergia a la penicilina?
¿Tiene usted alergia a la leche?
¿Tiene usted frío?
¿Tiene usted calor?
¿Tiene usted miedo?
¿Tiene usted sed?
¿Tiene usted hambre?
¿Cuántos años tiene usted?
¿Cuántos años tiene la niña?
¿Cuántos años tienen sus padres?
¿Tiene usted algo?
¿Tiene usted algo en el ojo?
No, no tengo nada en la mano.
No, no tengo nada en el esófago.

10.4
Yo muevo el vientre una vez/___ veces por día.

Yo orino __ veces por día.

Pepe orina en el inodoro.

Sí, Pepe orina en el inodoro siempre.

Sí, yo orino en el inodoro siempre.

Yo orino muchas veces por mes.

Sí, yo hago ejercicio con frecuencia/No, yo no hago ejercicio con frecuencia.

Sí, yo hago esfuerzo con frecuencia/No, yo no hago esfuerzo con frecuencia.

Sí, yo cambio la nitroglicerina a menudo.

Sí, yo cambio la nitroglicerina cada 6 a 12 meses.

¿Toma usted una tableta de nitroglicerina cada vez que usted tiene dolor de pecho?

Pepe estuvo en Hawaii.

Pepe nunca estuvo en Hawaii.

Pepe nunca estuvo enfermo.

Pepe tuvo fiebre.

Pepe nunca tuvo fiebre.

Pepe nunca tuvo angina.

Pepe nunca tuvo angina con el ejercicio.

Pepe nunca caminó al trabajo.

Pepe nunca caminó una milla.

Pepe nunca caminó una milla en su vida.

Pepe nunca escupió sangre.

Pepe nunca escupió sangre en su vida.

10.5
yo doy

él da

ella da

usted da

nosotros damos

ellos dan

ellas dan

ustedes dan

Yo doy el lápiz a Pepe.

Yo doy el lápiz a él.

Yo doy el lápiz a ella.

Yo doy el lápiz a usted.

Pepe da el lápiz a mí.

Yo doy los resultados a él.

El paciente da su número de seguro social.

El paciente da su número de seguro social a la recepcionista.

El paciente da su número de seguro a la recepcionista.

El paciente da su número de póliza a la secretaria.

El paciente da su número de póliza a la trabajadora social.

El paciente da la información a la trabajadora social.

10.6
Pepe me da el lápiz.
Pepe le da el lápiz.
Pepe le da el lápiz.
Pepe le da el lápiz.
Yo le doy el lápiz.
Yo le doy el lápiz.
Yo le doy el lápiz.
El paciente da.
El paciente me da.
El paciente me da el brazo.
El paciente le da.
El paciente le da la botella.
El paciente le da.
El paciente le da el número de seguro social.
El paciente le da.
El paciente le da su número de teléfono.
Yo doy.
Yo le doy.
Yo le doy un ataque al corazón.
Yo doy.
Yo le doy.
Yo le doy una inyección.
El da.
El me da.
El me da un ataque al corazón.
El le da una vacuna.
Deme el brazo, por favor.
Deme la receta, por favor.
Deme la permiso, por favor.
Deme el permiso correcto, por favor.

10.7
Yo tengo un dolor de cabeza.
¿Duele la cabeza?
me
Me duele la cabeza.
Le duele la cabeza.
Le duele el pecho.
Le duele el dedo.
¿Le duele la cabeza?
¿Le duele el tobillo?
¿Le duele el pecho?
¿Le quema la orina?
¿Le pica la vagina?
¿Le pica la erupción de la piel?
¿Le molesta la venda?
¿Le molesta el yeso?
¿Le gusta el chocolate?

¿Le gusta caminar?
¿Le gusta mirar la televisión?
¿Le gusta tener hijos?

Lesson 11

11.1
Yo voy al baño ___ veces por día.
Pepe va al baño 3 veces por día.
Pepita va al baño 4 veces por día.
Uste va al baño 5 veces por día.
Nosotros vamos al baño 12 veces por día.
Pepe y Pepita van al baño 7 veces por día.
Pepe: Usted va a comer una hamburguesa.
Pepe: Usted va a mirar la televisión hasta las 10:30.
Pepe: Usted va a dormir a las 11:00.
Usted va a dormir.
¿Va a dormir usted?
¿Va a comer mañana?
¿Va a evitar sal?
¿Va a evitar cosas peligrosas?
¿Va a trabajar con el yeso?
Usted va a mejorar.
El dolor va a mejorar.
El dolor va a empeorar.
El dolor en los dientes va a empeorar.
La enfermedad no va a empeorar.
Yo voy a mirar la televisíon.
Yo voy a sacar sangre.
Yo voy a sacar sangre de su brazo.
I am going to eat.
I am going to sleep.
Yo voy a comer.
Yo voy a dormir.

11.2
Pepe: Sí, tengo diarrea.
Pepe: Sí, tengo fiebre.
Pepe: Hace 3 días.
Pepe: Hace 3 días.
Ana: ¿Cuándo comenzó el dolor?
Pepe: Hace 2 días.
Ana: ¿Cuándo comenzó la alergia ?
Pepe: Hace 10 años.
Ana: ¿Cuándo tuvo la operación?
Pepe: Hace 5 años.
Ana: ¿Cuándo tuvo su último hijo?

Pepe: Hace 11 meses.
Ana: ¿Cuándo tuvo el accidente?
Pepe: Hace 1 hora.
Ana: ¿Cuándo comió?
Pepe: Hace 13 horas.
Ana: ¿Cuándo va a comer?
Pepe: En 15 minutos.
Ana: ¿Cuándo va a ir?
Pepe: En media hora.
Ana: ¿Cuándo va a comenzar el tratamiento?
Pepe: En 5 meses.
Ana: ¿Cuándo va a comenzar la operación?
Pepe: En media hora.

11.3
El paciente puede hablar español.
La madre del niño puede hablar inglés.
El paciente puede caminar con ayuda.
El hombre puede caminar un bloque.
¿Puede caminar un bloque?
¿Puede subir un piso?
¿Puede subir un escalón?
¿Cuántos escalones puede subir?
El paciente debe hacer ejercicio.
El paciente debe seguir una dieta estricta.
La madre del niño debe firmar el permiso.
El paciente quiere dormir.
El niño quiere quitar el abrigo.
El niño quiere poner la ropa.
¿Quiere usted ayuda?
El niño tiene que dormir.
La madre del niño tiene que firmar el permiso.
Primero, usted tiene que ir a la farmacia.
Primero, la sangre tiene que ir al corazón.
El corazón tiene que impulsar la sangre al resto del cuerpo.
La sangre tiene que ir a los riñones.
¿Tiene que dormir?
¿Tiene que dormir con tres almohadas?
El paciente trata de firmar el permiso.
El paciente trata de correr.
El corazón es una bomba.
El corazón es una bomba que trata de impulsar la sangre a los riñones.
Yo voy a tratar de quitar el dolor.
Yo voy a tratar de explicar.
Yo voy a tratar de explicar cómo el corazón impulsa la sangre.

El paciente no puede subir dos escalones.
La madre del niño no puede hablar español.
El paciente trata de subir dos escalones pero no puede.

Cuando el corazón no puede impulsar la sangre, se llama insuficiencia cardíaca.
No debe fumar.
No debe firmar el permiso antes de comprender la operación.
El niño no quiere quitar la ropa.
El niño no quiere poner la bata.
Usted no tiene que firmar el permiso.
¿No tiene que ir a la casa ahora?

Usted va a poder dormir.
Su madre va a querer ir.
Usted no va a tener que tener una operación.
El paciente va a tratar de caminar.

11.4
Pepe: Sí, para estar sano hay que comer bien.
Juan: Sí, para estar sano hay que hacer ejercicio.
Pepe: Sí, para estar sano hay que dormir 8 horas.
Juan: Sí, para estar sano hay que descansar.
Pepe: Sí, para estar sano hay que estar contento.
Pepe: No, para estar sano no hay que comer demasiado.

11.5
Pepe: Ella tiene que regresar a Cleveland, ¡si no yo voy a estar muy mal!
Pepe: Sí, ¡si no yo voy a morir de insuficiencia cardíaca!
Pepe: Sí, ¡si no yo voy a ir a vivir con Juan!

Lesson 12

12.1
Yo me lavo la cabeza.
Yo me despierto.
Yo me lavo la cara.
Yo me cepillo los dientes.
Yo me ducho.
Yo me seco la cara.
Yo me seco el pelo.
Yo me peino el pelo.
Yo me visto.
Yo me llamo Ana.
¿Cómo se llama usted?
¿Cómo se lava?
¿Cómo se lava la cara?
¿Cómo se ducha?
¿A qué hora se ducha?

Yo lavo.
Yo me lavo.

Yo me lavo la cara.
Yo lavo.
Yo lavo la cara de Pepe.
El cepilla.
El se cepilla.
El se cepilla los dientes.
El cepilla.
El cepilla el pelo del paciente.
Usted llama.
Usted se llama.
Usted se llama Juan.
Usted llama.
Usted llama al doctor.

12.2
(the sample sentences are only one of many possibilities that you might come up with)

verb	reflexive infinitive?	phrase
cepillar	cepillarse	Yo me cepillo los dientes.
despertar	despertarse	Ella se despierta a las 7.
duchar	ducharse	Yo me ducho a la mañana.
bañar	bañarse	El se baña a la noche.
querer	no	Usted quiere estudiar.
masticar	no	Yo mastico el chocolate.
hablar	no	Ella habla por teléfono.
secar	secarse	El se seca con la toalla.
rasurar	rasurarse	Usted se rasura la barba.
peinar	peinarse	Yo me peino el pelo.
acostar	acostarse	El niño se acuesta en la cama.
levantar	levantarse	La niña se levanta de la cama.
fumar	no	El paciente fuma un cigarrillo.
llamar	llamarse	Yo me llamo Ana.
respirar	no	Respire profundo, ¡por favor!
ahogar	ahogarse	El perro se ahogó en el agua.
correr	no	El doctor corre al cuarto.
mover	moverse	El bebé se mueve en el útero.
vestir	vestirse	Yo me visto a la mañana.
acumular	acumularse	El dinero se acumula en el banco.

12.3
¿Cómo se siente?
¿Se siente enfermo/a?
¿Se siente sano/a?
¿Se siente bien?
¿Se siente mal?
¿Se siente débil?
¿Se siente fuerte?

¿Se siente peor?
¿Se siente mejor?
¿Se siente triste?
¿Se siente contento/a?
¿Se siente deprimido/a?
¿Se siente cómo un paciente?
¿Se siente cómo si se ahoga?
¿Se siente cómo si se ahoga si usted duerme con una almohada?

12.3.1

Se lastima con el carro.
¿Se lastimó con el carro?
¿Cuándo se lastimó?
¿Cómo se lastimó?
¿A qué hora se lastimó?
¿Con qué se lastimó?
¿Porqué se lastimó?

12.3.2

lave
quite
quite
¡Quítese el sombrero, por favor!
¡Quítese la ropa, por favor!
¡Quítese el abrigo, por favor!
¡Quítese las joyas, por favor!
Quítese el pantalón.
¡Quítese todo, por favor!
Quítese todo de la cintura arriba.
Quítese todo de la cintura abajo.
acueste
¡Acuéstese en la cama, por favor!
¡Acuéstese boca arriba, por favor!
¡Acuéstese boca abajo, por favor!
Acuéstese en el lado derecho.
Acuéstese en el lado izquierdo.
¡Acuéstese aquí, por favor!
mueva
El niño se mueve.
El niño se mueve en la cama.
El bebé se mueve en el útero.
¡No se mueva, por favor!
¡Acuéstese y no se mueva, por favor!
ponga
Póngase la ropa.
Póngase los pantalones.
Póngase el abrigo.
Póngase la bata.
Póngase la ropa interior.

Póngase los anteojos.
Quítese la ropa.
Póngase la bata.
Acuéstese boca arriba.
¡Quítese la ropa, póngase la bata, y acuéstese boca arriba, por favor!

12.4
falta un diente
falta un botón
Falta el diente.
Falta el paciente.
Falta el resultado.
Falta el análisis.
Falta la receta.

Pepe tiene falta de aire.
¿Tiene Pepe falta de aire?
¿Tiene usted falta de aire?
¿Tiene usted falta de aire cuando camina?
¿Puede caminar dos bloques sin falta de aire?
¿Cuántos escalones puede subir sin falta de aire?
¿Tiene falta de aire a la noche?
¿Cuánto dura la falta de aire?
¿Se levanta a la noche?
¿Se tiene que levantar a la noche?
¿Se tiene que levantar a la noche para abrir la ventana?
¿Corre usted para abrir la ventana a la noche porque tiene falta de aire?

Appendix A. The Adult History

This appendix contains all the questions and answers in correct English and Spanish; tenses not taught in the Manual are also included.

THE ADULT HISTORY	LA HISTORIA CLINICA DEL ADULTO

(The English history has been taken, in part, from *A Guide to Physical Examination and History Taking*, 4th ed., Barbara Bates, J. B. Lippincott, 1987.)

IDENTIFYING DATA

How old are you?	¿Cuántos años tiene?
Where were you born?	¿Dónde nació?
Are you single?	¿Es soltero/a?
Are you married?	¿Está casado/a?
Are you divorced?	¿Está divorciado/a?
Are you widowed?	¿Es viudo/a?
Do you have children?	¿Tiene hijos?
Are you employed?	¿Está empleado?
Where do you work?	¿Dónde trabaja?
What is your religion?	¿Cuál es su religión?

PRESENT ILLNESS

What is the problem?	¿Cuál es el problema?
When did it begin?	¿Cuándo comenzó?
How did it begin?	¿Cómo comenzó?
What happened?	¿Qué ocurió?
What makes it worse?	¿Qué lo empeora?
What makes it better?	¿Qué lo mejora?
Do you have pain?	¿Tiene dolor?
For how long have you had pain?	¿Hace cuánto tiene dolor?
Is this the first time that you have this pain?	¿Es la primera vez que tiene este dolor?
When was the last time that you had this pain?	¿Cuándo fue la última vez que tuvo este dolor?
Where is the pain?	¿Dónde está el dolor?
What's the pain like?	¿Cómo es el dolor?
When do you have the pain?	¿Cuándo tiene el dolor?
When does it begin?	¿Cuándo comienza?
How long does it last?	¿Cuánto dura?

How often do you have it?	¿Con qué frecuencia tiene el dolor?
What makes the pain come?	¿Qué precipita el dolor?
What else happens when you get the pain?	¿Qué más le pasa cuando tiene el dolor?
What do you believe you have?	¿Qué cree que tiene usted?
Are you worried?	¿Está preocupado?
How has this problem affected	¿Qué consecuencias ha tenido este problema
your ability to work?	en su trabajo?
your life at home?	en su casa?
your social activities?	en sus actividades sociales?
your role as a parent?	en su rol de padre/madre?
your role as a spouse?	en su rol de esposo/esposa?
the way you feel about yourself?	en la forma en que usted piensa de sí mismo?
your sexual activities?	en su vida sexual?

PAST HISTORY

What would you say is your state of health?	¿Qué le parece el estado de su salud general en general?
Childhood illnesses (please see "Childhood Illnesses" Appendix "D" p. 237)	
What illnesses have you had as an adult?	¿Cuáles enfermedades ha tenido de adulto?
Do you have, or have you had, any psychiatric illnesses?	¿Tiene o ha tenido alguna enfermedad mental?
Have you ever had an accident or an injury?	¿Ha tenido un accidente o se ha lastimado?
Have you ever had an operation?	¿Ha tenido una operación?
Have you ever been in the hospital?	¿Ha estado hospitalizado?

CURRENT HEALTH STATUS

Do you have any allergies?	¿Tiene alergias?
Have you been immunized against	¿Ha tenido vacunas contra
tetanus	tétano
pertussis	tos ferina
diphtheria	difteria
polio	polio
measels	sarampión
rubella	rubela
mumps	paperas
influenza	gripe
hepatitis B	hepatitis B
Are there any environmental hazards in your home/school/ workplace?	¿Hay cosas tóxicas en su casa/escuela/lugar dónde trabaja?
Do you use a seat belt?	¿Usa usted el cinturón de seguro ?
How do you sleep at night?	¿Cómo duerme a la noche?

Do you have difficulty	¿Tiene dificultad
falling asleep	en dormirse
staying asleep	en quedarse dormido/a
getting up	en despertarse
What do you eat in a typical day?	¿Qué es lo que come en un día típico?
How much coffee/tea/caffeinated	¿Cuánto café, té, y otras bebidas con
drinks do you drink per day?	cafeína toma por día?
Do you take any medications?	¿Toma medicamentos?
Do you take any home remedies?	¿Toma medicamentos caseros?
Do you take nonprescription drugs?	¿Toma medicamentos sin receta?
Do you take any medications	¿Toma medicamentos que ha pedido
that you have borrowed	prestado de sus amigos
from friends or family?	o de su familia?
Do you smoke?	¿Fuma usted?
What do you smoke	¿Qué fuma
(cigarette, pipe, cigar)?	(cigarrillo, pipa, cigarro)?
How much do you smoke?	¿Cuánto fuma?
For how long have you been smoking?	¿Hace cuánto fuma?
Do you drink alcohol?	¿Toma usted bebidas alcohólicas?
How much do you drink per day?	¿Cuánto bebe usted por día?
What do you drink?	¿Qué bebe?
Do you take any recreational drugs?	¿Toma usted drogas ilícitas?
What do you take?	¿Cuáles drogas toma?
Do you use IV drugs?	¿Usa usted drogas endovenosas?
Have you ever used IV drugs?	¿Ha tomado drogas endovenosas alguna vez?

FAMILY HISTORY

(Please refer to "The Family" Appendix "F" p. 241 for the names of specific family members)

How old is your...?	¿Cuántos años tiene su...?
What is the health of your ... like?	¿Cómo es la salud de ...?
What did your ... die of?	¿De qué falleció (murió) su ...?
How old was ... when he died?	¿Cuántos años tenía ... cuando falleció?
In your family, is there a history of	¿Hay en su familia
diabetes	diabetes
tuberculosis	tuberculosis
heart disease	enfermedad del corazón
high blood pressure	presión alta
stroke	ataque cerebral
kidney disease	enfermedad de los riñones
cancer	cáncer
arthritis	artritis
anemia	anemia
headaches	dolor de cabeza
epilepsy	epilepsia
mental illness	enfermedad mental

symptoms like yours?   síntomas como los suyos?

PSYCHOSOCIAL HISTORY

Do you live alone or with someone else?   ¿Vive solo o con alguien?
With whom?   ¿Con quién vive?
Tell me a little about your family.   Cuénteme algo sobre su familia.
Are they here in the United States?   ¿Están ellos aquí en los Estados Unidos?
Where are they?   ¿Dónde están?
Where are you from?   ¿De dónde es usted?
Do you miss your country?   ¿Extraña usted a su país?
Was it difficult for you to   ¿Fue difícil irse de su país?
  leave your country?
How long have you been in this city?   ¿Hace cuánto está en esta ciudad?
In this country?   ¿En este país?
Do you have friends here?   ¿Tiene amigos aquí?
Are they American or are   ¿Son ellos norte americanos o son
  they from ____?   de _____?
Did you go to school in ___?   ¿Fue a la escuela en ___?
What grade did you complete?   ¿Hasta qué grado fue?
Did you serve in the army?   ¿Hizo el servicio militar?
What did you do in ____?   ¿Qué hacía en ____?
Did you work there?   ¿Trabajaba ahí?
What type of work did you do?   ¿Qué tipo de trabajo hacía?
Do you make enough money now   ¿Gana suficiente para sus
  to make ends meet?   gastos ahora?
Are you happy in your marriage?   ¿Está contento/a con su esposo/a?
Has immigrating been difficult for   ¿Ha sido difícil para
  you in your marriage?   ustedes la migración?
Does your wife/husband speak English?   ¿Habla inglés su esposo/a?
Does she/he work?   ¿Trabaja él/ella?
Does she/he have friends here?   ¿Tiene él/ella amigos aquí?
Do you have any hobbies?   ¿Tiene usted un pasatiempo favorito?
Are you retired?   ¿Está usted jubilado?
Do you go to church?   ¿Va usted a la iglesia?
Is religion important to you?   ¿Es la religión algo importante para usted?

REVIEW OF SYSTEMS

General
What is your usual weight?   ¿Cuánto pesa de costumbre?
Has there been a recent weight change?   ¿Ha cambiado de peso recientemente?
Do you feel weak? Fatigued?   ¿Se siente débil? Con fatiga?
(N.B. this can mean "are you tired"
or "do you have shortness of breath.")
Do you have a fever?   ¿Tiene fiebre?

Skin
Please see "Dermatology" in Appendix "D" p. 239

Head
Do you have headaches?	¿Tiene usted dolores de cabeza?
Have you had a head injury?	¿Se ha lastimado la cabeza?

Eyes
Do you wear glasses or contact lenses?	¿Usa usted anteojos o lentes de contacto?
When was your last eye exam?	¿Cuándo fue la última vez que fue al oculista?
Do you have	¿Tiene usted
pain	dolor
redness	ojos inflamados
excessive tearing	muchas lágrimas
double vision	visión doble
glaucoma	glaucoma
cataracts	cataratas

Ears
Do you have any problems with your hearing?	¿Tiene algún problema con el oído?
Do you have	¿Tiene usted
tinnitus	sonidos en los oídos
vertigo	mareos
earaches	dolor de oído
infection	infección en los oídos
discharge	flujo de los oídos

Nose and Sinuses
Do you have	¿Tiene usted
frequent colds	resfríos frecuentes
nasal stuffiness	la nariz constipada
discharge	flujo de la nariz
itchiness	picazón en la nariz
hay fever	fiebre de heno
nosebleeds	sangre de la nariz
sinus trouble	problemas de sinusitis

Mouth and Throat
What is the condition of your teeth and gums?	¿En qué condición están sus dientes y ancías?
Do you have bleeding gums?	¿Le sangran las ancías?
When was your last dental exam?	¿Cuándo fue la última vez que fue al dentista?

Do you have a sore tongue?	¿Le duele la lengua?
Do you have frequent sore throats?	¿Tiene usted dolor de garganta a menudo?
Do you have hoarseness?	¿Está usted afónico?

Neck

Do you have	¿Tiene usted
lumps	bultos
"swollen glands"	glándulas inflamadas
goiter	bocio
pain	dolor
stiffness	tortícolis
in your neck?	en su cuello?

Breasts

Do you have	¿Tiene usted
lumps	bultos
pain	dolor
discomfort	molestia
nipple discharge	flujo del pezón
Do you do your own self-breast exam?	¿Se examina usted sus pechos?

Respiratory

Do you have	¿Tiene usted
cough	tos
hempotysis	tos con sangre
wheezing	respiración con silbidos
asthma	asma
bronchitis	bronquitis
emphysema	enfisema
pneumonia	pulmonía/ neumonia
tuberculosis	tuberculosis
pleurisy	pleuresía
sputum	esputo
What color is the sputum?	¿De qué color es el esputo?
How much sputum do you have?	¿Cuánto esputo tiene?
When was the last time that	¿Cuándo fue la última vez que
you had a chest X-ray taken?	se sacó una radiografía del pecho?

Cardiac

Do you have	¿Tiene usted
heart trouble	problemas del corazón
high blood pressure	presión alta
rheumatic fever	fiebre reumática
heart murmurs	soplo
chest pain or discomfort	dolor oolestia de pecho

palpitations
dyspnea
orthopnea
paroxsysmal nocturnal dyspnea

edema
Have you had an ECG before or
other cardiac tests?

palpitaciones
respiración dificil
respiración dificil al recostarse
la sensasión de ahogarse cuando se recuesta
a la noche
edema
¿Ha tenido un electrocardiograma u
otros exámenes cardíacos ?

Gastrointestinal

Do you have
trouble swallowing
heartburn
change in your appetite
nausea
vomiting
regurgitation
hematemesis
indigestion
How frequently do you have
a bowel movement?
What color is your stool?
What size is your stool?
Have you had a change in your
bowel habits?
Do you have
rectal bleeding
black tarry stools
hemorrhoids
constipation
diarrhea
abdominal pain
food intolerance
excessive belching
excessive passing of gas
jaundice
liver trouble
gallbladder trouble
hepatitis

¿Tiene usted
problemas cuando traga
acidez
un cambio en su apetito
nausea
vómitos
regurgitación
vómitos con sangre
indigestión
¿Cuántas veces mueve usted el
vientre?
¿De qué color es su excremento?
¿De qué tamaño es su excremento?
¿Ha cambiado la manera en la cual
usted mueve el vientre?
¿Tiene usted
sangre por el ano
excremento negro
hemorroides
estreñimiento
diarrea
dolor de estómago
alergia a alguna comida
muchos eructos
mucho gas
ictericia
problemas con el hígado
problemas con la vesícula
hepatitis

Urinary

How frequently do you urinate?
Do you have polyuria?
Do you have nocturia?
Do you have burning or pain
on urination?
Do you have hematuria?

¿Cuántas veces orina usted?
¿Orina usted demasiado?
¿Se levanta usted a la noche para orinar?
¿Le pica o le duele cuando orina?

¿Tiene usted sangre en la orina?

Do you have urgency?	¿Tiene usted muchas ganas de orinar?
Do you have reduced caliber or force of the urinary stream?	¿Tiene menos cantidad de orina o menos fuerza cuando orina?
Do you have hesitancy?	¿Le es difícil comenzar a orinar?
Do you have incontinence?	¿Es usted incontinente?
Do you have urinary infections?	¿Tiene usted infecciones de la orina?
Do you have stones?	¿Tiene usted cálculos?

Genitoreproductive System in Men

Do you have	¿Tiene usted
hernias	hernias
discharge from the penis	flujo del pene
sore on your penis	llagas en el pene
testicular pain	dolor en los testículos
testicular masses	bultos en los testículos
Have you ever had a venereal disease?	¿Ha tenido una enfermedad venérea?
Which ones?	¿Cuáles?
Were you treated for them?	¿Le dieron algún tratamiento?
Are you sexually active?	¿Tiene relaciones sexuales?
How is your sexual function?	¿Cómo funciona sexualmente?
Are you satisfied sexually?	¿Está satisfecho sexualmente?
Do you have any sexual problems?	¿Tiene algún problema sexual?
Do you have more than one sexual partner?	¿Tiene usted relaciones sexuales con más de una persona?
Do you have intercourse with men/women/both?	¿Tiene usted relaciones sexuales con hombres/mujeres/ambos?

Genitoreproductive System in Women

At what age did you get your period?	¿A qué edad empezó la regla/ la menstruación/el período?
How regular are your periods?	¿Son regulares o no sus períodos?
How frequently do you get one?	¿Cada cuánto tiene un período?
How long do they last?	¿Cuántos días dura?
How much bleeding do you have?	¿Cuánta sangre tiene cuando tiene el período?
Do you have	¿Tiene usted
dysmenorrhea	períodos dolorosos
premenstrual tension	tensión antes de tener el período
At what age did you start menopause?	¿Cuántos años tenía cuando le vino la menopausia?
What menopausal symptoms did you have?	¿Cuáles fueron los síntomas que tuvo cuando le vino la menopausia?
Have you had any postmenopausal bleeding?	¿Tuvo sangre por la vagina después de comenzar la menopausia?
Do you have	¿Tiene usted
discharge	flujo
itching	picazón
sores	llagas

lumps	bultos
veneral diseases	enfermedades venéreas
How many times have you been pregnant?	¿Cuántas veces ha estado embarazada?
How many times have you delivered?	¿Cuántos partos ha tenido?
Have you had an abortion? (Spontaneous or induced)	¿Ha tenido un aborto? (Malparto o aborto)
How many?	¿Cuántos?
Did you have any complications when you were pregnant?	¿Tuvo alguna complicación cuando estuvo embarazada?
Do you use any birth control?	¿Usa algún método de contracepción?
(See above for sexual history)	
Do you have dyspareunia?	¿Tiene usted dolor cuando tiene relaciones sexuales?

Peripheral Vascular

Do you have	¿Tiene usted
intermittent claudication	dolor en las piernas cuando camina
leg cramps	calambres en las piernas
varicose veins	várices
thrombophlebitis	flebitis

Musculoskeletal

Please see "Rheumatology" Appendix "D" p. 240

Neurologic

Do you faint?	¿Se desmaya usted?
Do you have blackouts?	¿Pierde usted el conocimiento?
Do you have	¿Tiene usted
seizures	convulsiones
weakness	debilidad
paralysis	parálisis
numbness	entumecimiento
tingling	hormigueo
tremors or other involuntary movements	temblor u otros movimientos involuntarios

Hematologic

Do you have anemia?	¿Tiene usted anemia?
Do you have easy bruising?	¿Se le hacen moretones fácilmente?
Do you have easy bleeding?	¿Sangra fácilmente?
Have you had a past blood transfusion?	¿Le han dado una transfusión de sangre antes?
Have you ever had a reaction to a blood transfusion?	¿Ha tenido una reacción a una transfusión de sangre?

Endocrine

Do you have
   thyroid trouble
   heat or cold intolerance
   excessive sweating
   diabetes
   excessive thirst or hunger
Do you have polyuria?

¿Tiene usted
   problemas de la tiroide
   intolerancia al calor o al frío
   mucho sudor
    diabetes
   mucha hambre o sed
¿Tiene usted que orinar mucho?

Psychiatric

Are you nervous?
Do you have much tension?
How would you describe your mood?
How is your memory?

¿Está usted nerviosa?
¿Tiene usted mucha tensión?
¿Cómo está de ánimo?
¿Cómo está de la memoria?

Appendix B. The Pediatric History

THE PEDIATRIC HISTORY   LA HISTORIA CLINICA DEL NIÑO

(taken from the patient's mother of a male patient)

BIRTH HISTORY

Prenatal

What was your health like before
  and during the pregnancy?
Did you have to take any drugs
  during the pregnancy?
Did you gain much weight?
Did you have any vaginal bleeding?
How many months did the pregnancy last?
Did you want to get pregnant?

¿Cómo estaba de salud antes y
  durante el embarazo?
¿Tuvo que tomar medicamentos
  durante el embarazo?
¿Aumentó mucho de peso?
¿Sangró de la vagina?
¿Cuántos meses duró el embarazo?
¿Usted quizo quedar embarazada?

Natal

How was the labor and delivery?
Did you use any drugs?
Any complications?
Did you have twins, triplets or more?
His birth order?
His weight at birth?

¿Cómo fue el parto?
¿Tomó medicamentos durante el parto?
¿Tuvo alguna complicación?
¿Tuvo mellizos, trillizos o más?
¿Qué número fue él?
¿Cuánto pesó él cuando nació?

Neonatal

Did he have difficulty taking
  his first breath?
Any problems with feeding?
Did he have
  respiratory distress
  cyanosis
  jaundice
  anemia
  convulsions
  congenital anomalies
  infection
How was your health postpartum?

Were you separated from the

¿Tuvo problemas con la primera
  respiración?
¿Tuvo problemas para comer?
¿Tuvo él
  problemas respiratorios
  piel azul
  ictericia (piel amarilla)
  anemia
  convulsiones
  anormalidades congénitas
  una infección
¿Cómo se sintió de salud después del
  parto?

¿Estuvo separada del bebé por alguna

baby for any reason?	razón?
How were his patterns of	¿Cómo
crying	lloraba
sleeping	dormía
urination	orinaba
defecation	defecaba

FEEDING HISTORY

Infancy

Did you breast feed?	¿Le dió el pecho?
Are you breast feeding?	¿Le está dando el pecho?
How frequently?	¿Cada cuánto le da el pecho?
How long do the sessions last?	¿Cuánto tiempo le da?
Do you use formula?	¿Usa mamadera?
Are there any problems?	¿Hay algún problema?
When did you start to wean him?	¿Cuándo empezó a destetar al bebé?
Did you give him a bottle?	¿Le dió una mamadera?
Are you giving him formula?	¿Le está dando una mamadera?
What kind?	¿Qué tipo de formula?
Does it have iron?	¿Es con hierro?
Does he have	¿Tiene él
colic	cólicos
regurgitation	regurgitación
vomiting	vómitos
diarrhea	diarrea
Did you give him vitamins?	¿Le dió vitaminas?
Are you giving him vitamins?	¿Le está dando vitaminas?
What kind?	¿Qué tipo de vitaminas?
How much? How often?	¿Cuántas? ¿Cada cuánto?
Is he eating solid food?	¿Está comiendo comida?
When did you first introduce him?	¿Cuántos años tenía cuando comenzó?
Where there any problems?	¿Tuvo algun problema con la comida?
Allergic reactions?	¿Tuvo alguna reacción alérgica a la comida?
When did he start self-feeding?	¿Cuándo comenzó a comer solo?
Are there any problems with feeding?	¿Hay algun problema con la comida?

GROWTH AND DEVELOPMENTAL HISTORY

Physical Growth

Do you know his weight at	¿Sabe cuánto pesaba
birth	cuando nació
1 year	al año
2 years	a los 2 años
5 years	a los 5 años
10 years	a los 10 años

Developmental Milestones

How old was he when he	¿A qué edad levantó
held his head up while prone	la cabeza mientras acostado
rolled over	se dió vuelta
sat with support	se sentó con ayuda
sat alone	se sentó solo
stood with support	se puso de pie con ayuda
stood alone	se puso de pie solo
walked with support	caminó con ayuda
walked alone	caminó solo
said his first word	dijo la primera palabra
said combinations of words	dijo varias palabras
said sentences	dijo una frase
tied his own shoes	se ató los zapatos
dressed without help	se vistió sin ayuda

Social Development

How does he sleep?	¿Cómo duerme?
Where does he sleep?	¿Dónde duerme?
Does he have	¿Tiene él
nightmares	pesadillas
terror	miedo
Does he have somnambulation?	¿Es él sonámbulo?
Is he toilet trained?	¿Va al baño solo?
How did you train him?	¿Cómo lo entrenaron?
Does he have enuresis?	¿Se hace pis en la cama?
Does he have encopresis?	¿Defeca involuntariamente?
Does the child have problems speaking?	¿Tiene el niño problemas para hablar?
Does he stutter?	¿Tartamudéa él?
Does he baby talk?	¿Habla como un bebé?
Does he lisp?	¿Habla con ceceo?
About how many words would you say are in his vocabulary?	¿Más o menos cuántas palabras tiene él en su vocabulario?
Does he have head banging?	¿Se golpea la cabeza?
Does he have tics?	¿Tiene un tic?
Does he have thumb sucking?	¿Se chupa el dedo?
Does he have nailbiting?	¿Se come las uñas?
Does he have pica?	¿Come barro o pintura?
Does he have ritualistic behavior?	¿Tiene gestos repetidos?
How would you asses his temperament?	¿Cómo le parece su temperamento?
His response to discipline?	¿Cómo responde él a la disciplina?
How do you discipline him?	¿Cómo lo disciplinan a él?
Does he have temper tantrums?	¿Tiene él pataletas?
Does he have negativism?	¿Es él muy negativo?
Does he have withdrawal?	¿Es él muy introvertido?
Does he have aggressive behavior?	¿Es él muy agresivo?

Did he/Does he go to	¿Fue/Va él a
day care	un niñero
nursery school	un kindergarten
kindergarten	un kindergarten
school	a la escuela
How old was he when he went to (above)?	¿Cuántos meses/años tenía él cuando fue a ....
Do you like his (above)?	¿Le gusta a usted el.... de su niño?
Does he like his (above)?	¿Le gusta a él el ....
How is he doing in (above)?	¿Cómo anda ahí?
What are his grades like?	¿Cómo son sus notas?
Are there any school concerns?	¿Estáusted preocupada por algo escolar?
What are his relations with members of the opposite sex?	¿Cómo se lleva él con los chicos del otro sexo?
Is he inquisitive about	¿Es él curioso sobre
conception	la concepción
girl-boy differences	la diferencia entre las niñas y los niños
pregnancy	el embarazo
How do you feel about his questions about sex?	¿Cómo se siente usted cuando él le hace esas preguntas sobre la sexualidad?
Have you educated him about	¿Lo ha educado usted sobre
sex	la sexualidad
masturbation	la masturbación
nocturnal emissions	las emisiones nocturnas
development of secondary sexual characteristics	las características sexuales secundarias
sexual urges	ganas de tener relaciones sexuales
Does he date?	¿Sale él con chicas?
How independent is he?	¿Es o no independiente?
How is his relationship with	¿Cómo se lleva él con
you	usted
his father	con su padre
his siblings	con sus hermanos
his peers	con sus amigos
Does he have any	¿Tiene él
hobbies	un pasatiempo favorito
interests outside of school	intereses fuera de la escuela
Does he have any special friends (real or imaginary)?	¿Tiene él amigos especiales (de la realidad o de la imaginación)?
What are his major assests?	¿Cuáles son sus mejores calidades?
What are his best skills?	¿Cuáles son sus mejores capacidades?
What is his self-image?	¿Qué piensa él de si mismo?

(Please refer to "The Adult History" for the rest of the History and Review of Systems.)

Appendix C. The Physical Exam

THE PHYSICAL EXAM

EL EXAMEN FISICO

Initial instructions

Enter, please.
Sit down, please.
Take off your clothes and
  put on this gown with
  the opening to the back.
Lie down on your back.
Lie down on your stomach.

Entre, por favor.
Siéntese, por favor.
Quítese la ropa y
  póngase esta bata con
  la abertura hacia atrás.
Acuéstese boca arriba.
Acuéstese boca abajo.

Eye exam

Sit up, please.
I'm going to turn off the lights.
Look straight ahead.
Don't blink, please.
Try not to move, please.
Look to the right.
Look to the left.
Look up.
Look down.
Look at my nose and tell me
  when you can see my fingers.
Can you read this?

Siéntese, por favor.
Voy a apagar las luces.
Mire adelante.
No pestañee, por favor.
Trate de no moverse, por favor.
Mire a la derecha.
Mire a la izquierda.
Mire hacia arriba.
Mire hacia abajo.
Mire mi nariz y dígame cuándo
  puede ver mis dedos.
¿Puede leer esto?

Ear

I'm going to put this instrument
  in your ear. This will not hurt.
Can you hear this?
Tell me when you stop hearing this.

Voy a poner este instrumento en
  su oído. No le va a doler.
¿Escucha esto?
Dígame cuando no lo escucha más.

Nose

I'm going to put this instrument
  in your nose. This will not hurt.
Breathe in.
What does this smell like?
Does it hurt when I tap here?

Voy a poner este instrumento en
  su nariz. No le va a doler.
Respire.
¿A qué huele esto?
¿Le duele si le golpeo aquí?

Throat

Please take off your dentures.	Por favor, quítese la dentadura postiza.
Please open your mouth, stick out your tongue, and say AHHHH.	Por favor, abra la boca, saque la lengua y diga AAAAA.
Put your tongue against the roof of your mouth.	Ponga la lengua contra el cielo de la boca.
Bite down hard.	Muerda con fuerza.

Neck

I'm going to feel your neck for masses.	Voy a tocarle el cuello a ver si siento algun bulto.
Please swallow.	Por favor, trague.

Back

Does it hurt when I tap over your lower back?	¿Le duele si le golpeo aquí, sobre la cintura?

Chest

Please breathe in deeply, I'm going to listen to your lungs.	Por favor, inspire profundo, voy a auscultarle los pulmones.
Hold your breath.	Por favor, no respire.
Say EEEEE.	Diga iiiii.
Say 99.	Diga noventa y nueve.
Cough, please.	Tosa, por favor.

Musculoskeletal

(Please see "Rheumatology" Appendix "D" p. 240)

Breasts

I am going to examine your breasts.	Voy a examinarle los pechos.
Please hold your arms up, like this.	Por favor, ponga los brazos arriba, así.
Please put your hands on your waist, like this.	Por favor, ponga las manos en la cintura, así.
Please lie down.	Por favor, acuéstese.

Cardiovascular

Please turn your head to the other side.	Por favor, de vuelta la cabeza al otro lado.
My stethoscope is cold, I'm sorry.	Mi estetoscopio está frío, lo siento.
I'm going to listen to your heart.	Voy a auscultarle el corazón.
Please turn a little on your left side.	Por favor, vuéltese un poco al lado izquierdo.

Please sit forward.	Por favor, siéntese un poco inclinado hacia adelante.
Please breathe out.	Por favor, expire.

Abdomen

I'm going to examine your abdomen.	Voy a examinarle el abdomen.
Does this hurt?	¿Le duele esto?

Inguinal Area

I'm going to feel the lymph nodes in your inguinal area.	Voy a tocar los ganglios linfáticos en la ingle.
Does this hurt?	¿Le duele esto?

Genital and Rectal Examination in Men

I need to do a genital exam.	Necesito hacer el exámen de los genitales.
Please cough.	Por favor, tosa.
I need to do a rectal examination.	Necesito hacer el exámen del recto.
I know that it is unpleasant.	Sé que es desagradable.
Please lie on your left side with your legs bent up to your chest.	Por favor, acuéstese en su lado izquierdo con las rodillas dobladas y que toquen el pecho.
Please stand next to the bed.	Por favor, póngase de pie al lado de la cama.
Rest your torso on the bed.	Acuéste el torso encima de la cama.
You will feel my fingers and the jelly.	Va a sentir los dedo míos y la jalea.
Please push out while I insert my finger.	Por favor, haga fuerza mientras yo introduzco el dedo.

Pelvic Examination in Women

Please, put your feet in the stirrups.	Por favor, pónga los pies en los estribos.
Please, scoot all the way to the edge of the table.	Por favor, arrímese más aquí.
Relax your legs.	Relaje las piernas.
This is the temperature of the speculum.	Esta es la temperatura del espéculo.
You will feel my fingers now.	Ahora va a sentir mis dedos.
Does this hurt?	¿Le duele esto?
I am taking out the speculum.	Estoy sacando el espéculo.
I am going to insert two fingers in your vagina to do a manual exam.	Voy a introducir dos dedos míos en su vagina para hacer el examen manual.
I am going to insert one finger in your rectum to do a rectal exam.	Voy a introducir un dedo en su recto para hacer el examen del recto.

All done.	¡Ya terminanos!
You can scoot back.	Puede arrimarse más ahí.

Neurologic Exam

Can you smell this?	¿Puede oler esto?
Can you read this?	¿Puede leer esto?
Plese look to the right, to the left, up, and down.	Por favor, mire a la derecha, a la izquierda, arriba, y abajo.
Can you feel this?	¿Puede sentir esto?
Close you eyes as tightly as possible.	Cierre los ojos lo más posible.
Bite down hard.	Muerda con los dientes lo más posible.
Can you smile?	¿Puede sonreírse?
Can you taste this?	¿Qué gusto tiene esto?
Do you hear this?	¿Puede oir esto?
Open your moth wide and stick your tongue out.	Por favor, abra la boca bien grande y saque la lengua.
Push against my hand.	Haga fuerza contra mi mano.
Shrug your shoulders.	Encójase de hombros, por favor.
Please get up.	Levántese, por favor.
Stand up straight.	Póngase derecho.
Walk to the door.	Camine hacia la puerta.
Walk on your tip toes.	Camine en punta de pie.
Walk on your heels.	Camine con los talones.
Stand on one foot.	Levante un pie.
Stand on the other foot.	Ahora, levante el otro pie.
Hop on one foot.	Salte en un pie.
Bend your knees.	Doble las rodillas.
Hold on to my fingers and squeeze as hard as you can.	Agarre mis dedos y aprete lo más fuerte posible.
Pull against my hand.	Tire hacia usted.
Close your eyes.	Cierre los ojos.
Please try to stand while I push against you.	Por favor, trate de no moverse mientras yo lo empujo.
Put your hands out in front of you.	Extienda los brazos.
With this finger, touch the tip of your nose.	Con este dedo, tóquese la punta de la nariz.
You can get back on the bed.	Puede volver a la cama.
Can you feel this?	¿Siente esto?
Does this feel sharp or dull?	¿Es agudo o sordo?
Does this feel like two pins or one?	¿Son dos alfileres o una?
What does this feel like?	¿Qué sensación tiene?
Like a vibration?	¿Cómo una vibración?
Thank you very much.	Muchas gracias.
We are through with the physical exam.	Hemos terminado el examen físico.

Appendix D. Specialized Vocabulary

Dermatology

abcess	el absceso
acne	el acne
blister (n.)	la ampolla
boil	el forúnculo
bruise (n.)	el moretón
bulla	la ampolla grande
bump (n.)	el chichón
callus	el callo
chancre	el chancro
chicken pox	la varicela
complexion	el cutis
corn	el callo
crack (v.)	abrirse
cyst	el quiste
dandruff	la caspa
eczema	el eczema
flea	la pulga
freckles	la peca
German measels	la rubéola
hay fever	fiebre del heno
heal (itself)	curarse
hives	la urticaria
injury	la herida
itch (v.)	picar
itching (n.)	la picazón
lesion	la lesión
lice	los piojos
lump	el bulto
measels	el sarampión
mole	el lunar
pimple	el grano
psoriasis	la psoriasis
pus	el pus
raised	levantado/subido sobre la superficie de la piel
rash	la erupción; el salpullido
red streak	la línea/la raya roja
redness	la piel roja/rojiza
scab (n.)	la costra

scabies	la sarna
scale (n.)	la escama
scale (v.)	escamarse
scar (n.)	la cicatriz
scar (v.)	formarse una cicatriz/cicatrizarse
scratch (v.)	rascarse
sore (adj.)	sensible
sore (n.)	la llaga; la úlcera
swelling (n.)	el hinchazón
swollen	hinchado
tender	sensible
ulcer	la úlcera
vesicle	la ampolla
warts	la verruga
weeping	supurante
wheal	la roncha

Infectious Diseases

malaria	malaria
polio	polio
scarlet fever	fiebre escarlatina
tuberculosis	tuberculosis
typhoid	tifoidea
yellow fever	fiebre amarilla

Rheumatology

nouns

blood clot	el coágulo
bone	el hueso
calf	la pantorrilla
cartilage	el cartílago
discharge	el flujo
edema	el edema
gonorrhea	la gonorrea
gout	la gota
heel	el talón
hip	la cadera
joint	la articulación; la conjuntura
knee	la rodilla
ligament	el ligamento
muscle	el músculo
rheumatic fever	la fiebre reumática
shoulder	el hombro
tip toes	las puntas de los pies
toes	los dedos del pie

varicose veins   las várices

verbs
to buckle   doblar
to climb   subir
to comb   peinarse
to exercise   hacer ejercicio
to flex   doblar
to go down   bajar
to kneel   ponerse de rodillas
to lift   levantar
to snap   crujir
to squat   ponerse en cuclillas
to touch your toes   tocar los dedos del pie
to walk on your heels   caminar en los talones
to walk on your tip toes   caminar en las puntas de los pies

adjectives
deformed   deformado/a
dislocated   dislocado/a
discolored   con distinto color
heavy   pesado/a
like pins and needles   como hormigueo
numb   entumecido/a
red   rojo/a
swollen   hinchado/a
tender   sensible
warm   caliente

The Newborn   **El Recién Nacido**

breast feeding   **amamantar**
bottle   la mamadera
breast   el pecho
                                        el seno
breast feed   dar el pecho
                                        alimentar a pecho
                                        amamantar
                                        mamar
breast pump   la bomba para extraer leche
bra   el corpiño
nipple   el pezón
to pump milk   extraer la leche
to squeeze   apretar
to suck   chupar

how to burp the baby	**como eructar al bebé**
burp	eructar
cry	llorar
hiccough	tener hipo
pat	dar golpecitos
put on his stomach	poner boca abajo
rub the back	frotar la espalda
sit on the lap	sentar en la falda
touch	tocar
yawn	bostezar

Childhood Illnesses

chicken pox	la varicela
measels	la sarampión
mumps	las paperas
smallpox	la viruela
rheumatic fever	la fiebre reumática
rubella	la rubéola
whooping cough	la tos ferina

Appendix E. Pain

The English vocabulary on "pain" is taken from *Manual of History Taking, Physical Examination and Record Keeping,* Elmer Raus and Madonna Raus, J. B. Lippincott Co., 1974.

THE PAIN IS	EL DOLOR ES
abrupt	repentino
aching	doloroso
acute	agudo
beating	palpitante; latiente
boring	penetrante
burning	ardiente; como una quemadura
chronic	crónico
circumscribed	con límites
colicky	espasmódico; como cólicos
constant	constante
constricting	como una opresión
continuous	contínuo
cramping	como un calambre
darting	fulgurante; dolor vivo y repentino; como una punzada
diffused	general; sin límites
dull	sordo
excrutiating	insoportable
fixed	fijo
fulgurant	(see darting)
gas	gas
generalized	(see diffused)
girdle	sensación de un cinturón o una faja apretada
gnawing	como un retortijón
gripping	lo único que piensa es en el dolor
gradual	gradual
growing pain	dolor producido por el crecimiento
hunger	hambre
hurting	dolorido (to be painful); herido (to be injured)
intense	intenso
intermittent	intermitente; va y viene
localized	con límites
moderate	moderado
neuralgic	neurálgico

piercing	como una puñalada
pins and needles	hormigueo
pounding	(see beating)
radiating	que se extiende; que se difunde
referred	dolor que origina en una parte pero que se siente en otra
remittent	remitente
severe	severo
sharp	agudo
shifting	movedizo
shock-like	como un relámpago
sore	sensible
spasmodic	espasmódico
squeezing	como una opresión
stabbing	(see piercing)
steady	constante
stinging	que quema
stitches	puntadas
terebrant	(see piercing)
throbbing	(see beating)
tight	(see squeezing)
vague discomfort	molestia incómoda

Appendix F. The Family

THE FAMILY

THE FAMILY	LA FAMILIA
aunt	la tía
aunts and uncles	los tíos
brother	el hermano
brother-in-law	el cuñado
brothers and sisters	los hermanos
cousin, f.	la prima
cousin, m.	el primo
cousins	los primos
daddy	el papá; papi
daughter	la hija
daughter-in-law	la nuera
father	el padre
father-in-law	el suegro
godfather	el padrino
godmother	la madrina
grandfather	el abuelo
grandmother	la abuela
granddaughter	la nieta
grandparents	los abuelos
grandson	el nieto
half brother	el medio hermano
half sister	la media hermana
in-laws	los suegros
mommy	la mamá; mami
mother	la madre
mother-in-law	la suegra
nephew	el sobrino
niece	la sobrina
parents	los padres
sister	la hermana
son	el hijo
son-in-law	el yerno
stepbrother	el hermanastro
stepdaughter	la hijastra
stepfather	el padrastro
stepmother	la madrastra
stepsister	la hermanastra
stepson	el hijastro
uncle	el tío

Appendix G. The Calendar

DAYS OF THE WEEK   DIAS DE LA SEMANA

DAYS OF THE WEEK	DIAS DE LA SEMANA
Monday	el lunes
Tuesday	el martes
Wednesday	el miércoles
Thursday	el jueves
Friday	el viernes
Saturday	el sábado
Sunday	el domingo

N.B. We don't capitalize the days of the week in Spanish and we use the definite article, which is always masculine.

MONTHS OF THE YEAR   MESES DEL AÑO

MONTHS OF THE YEAR	MESES DEL AÑO
January	enero
February	febrero
March	marzo
April	abril
May	mayo
June	junio
July	julio
August	agosto
September	septiembre
October	octubre
November	noviembre
December	diciembre

N.B. We don't capitalize the months of the year, either, but we don't use articles with them.

SEASONS OF THE YEAR   ESTACIONES DEL AÑO

SEASONS OF THE YEAR	ESTACIONES DEL AÑO
the spring	la primavera
the summer	el verano
the autumn	el otoño
the winter	el invierno

Appendix H. Conjugation Tables

THE PRESENT

	-ar	-er	-ir
yo	-o	-o	-o
tú	-as	-es	-es
él / ella / usted	-a	-e	-e
nosotros	-amos	-emos	-imos
ellos / ellas / ustedes	-an	-en	-en

THE PRETERIT

	-ar	-er and -ir
yo	-é	-í
tú	-aste	-iste
él / ella / usted	-ó	-ió
nosotros	-amos	-imos
ellos / ellas / ustedes	-aron	-ieron

THE IMPERATIVE

	-ar	-er and -ir
tú	-a	-e
él / ella / usted	-e	-a
nosotros	-emos	-amos
ellos / ellas / ustedes	-en	-an

THE IMPERFECT (CONTINUOUS PAST)

	-ar	-er and -ir
yo	-aba	-ía
tú	-abas	-ías
él / ella / usted	-aba	-ía
nosotros	-abamos	-íamos
ellos / ellas / ustedes	-aban	-ían

THE FUTURE INDICATIVE

	-ar, -er and -ir
yo	-é
tú	-ás
él / ella / usted	-á
nosotros	-emos
ellos / ellas / ustedes	-án

THE CONDITIONAL

	-ar, -er and -ir
yo	-ía
tú	-ías
él / ella / usted	-ía
nosotros	-íamos
ellos / ellas / ustedes	-ían

THE PRESENT OF "ESTAR," "SER," "IR," AND "TENER"

	estar	ser	ir	tener
yo	estoy	soy	voy	tengo
tú	estás	eres	vas	tienes
él ella usted	está	es	va	tiene
nosotros	estamos	somos	vamos	tenemos
ellos ellas ustedes	están	son	van	tienen

THE PRETERIT OF "ESTAR," "SER," "IR," AND "TENER"

	estar	ser and ir	tener
yo	estuve	fui	tuve
tú	estuviste	fuiste	tuviste
él ella usted	estuvo	fue	tuvo
nosotros	estuvimos	fuimos	tuvimos
ellos ellas ustedes	estuvieron	fueron	tuvieron